THE
NICARAGUAN
EPIC

KATABASIS

CANTO EPICO TO THE FSLN

Song Cycle
by Carlos and Luis Enrique
Mejía Godoy

NICARAGUAN VISION
AND OTHER POEMS

by Julio Valle-Castillo

translated by Dinah Livingstone

First published 1989 by:
Katabasis
10 St Martins Close, London NW1 OHR

Distributed by:
Central Books, 14 The Leathermarket, London SE1 3ER
01-407 5447

ISBN 0 904872 12 2

Designed and Typeset by Boldface, 01-253 2014, London EC1
Printed by Short Run Press, 0296 631075
Cover Design: Boldface. The cover photo shows Germán Pomares, 'El Danto' (centre) with comrades in the mountains shortly before his death. Illustrations to 'Nicaragua Nicaragüita' and 'The Birth': John Kingsley Cook.

Most of the photos were sent from Nicaragua by Julio Valle-Castillo
Photos on pages 90, 128, 129: Susan Meiselas.

Julio Valle-Castillo is a well known Nicaraguan poet born in Masaya, in 1952. His collections include *Las Armas iniciales* (Mexico 1977) and *Formas Migratorias* (Mexico 1979). Since the Revolution of 1979 he has worked with Ernesto Cardenal in the Ministry of Culture and is the editor of its magazine, *Poesía Libre*. He is also on the editorial board of *Nuevo Amanecer Cultural*, the weekly supplement to the newspaper *El Nuevo Diario*. On a visit to England in 1987 he wrote a long poem about the Kings Cross fire. The poems translated here are taken from his most recent collection *Materia Jubilosa* (Managua 1986).

The brothers Carlos and Luis Enrique Mejía Godoy are Nicaragua's foremost poet-musicians who, with their respective bands, Los de Palacaguina and Ocotal, have travelled the world singing their revolutionary songs, many of which became familiar to their compatriots in the dictator Somoza's time, when singing them was a subversive act. Some of these famous songs are recorded on *Guitarra Armada*. The *Canto Epico to the FSLN* was first performed at a festival in East Germany in 1981.

The Nicaragua Solidarity Campaign, 23 Bevenden Street, London N1 (01-253 0246) sell the *Canto Epico* on cassette and other recordings by the Mejía Godoy brothers.

A live recording of Carlos's *Nicaraguan Mass* (Misa Campesina), in Spanish and English, made in London in 1986, together with the Spanish text and translation by Dinah Livingstone (published by CIIR) is also available from the Nicaragua Solidarity Campaign.

ACKNOWLEDGMENTS

I'd like to thank all those who helped me with this book. As well as the authors, I'd like to thank the singers Humberto Quintanilla, Silvio Linarte and Enrique Duarte for transcriptions and explanations; Maria Carmen Pérez Zelaya, who showed me round the Managua Armed Forces Museum, and the Instituto de Estudio del Sandinismo who gave me useful material. In Managua I'd also like to thank Alun Burge of CIIR, and naturalists Cindy Taft and Mauricio Araquistain. In London I'd like to thank Sandro Peñalba of the Nicaraguan Embassy, the library staff at London Zoo and Kew Gardens and Dale Russell of Boldface, the book's imaginative and meticulous designer.

Dinah Livingstone

MAP OF NICARAGUA

HONDURAS

R. COCO

R. BOCAY

Mozonte   El Chipote

Somoto

Esteli   Jinotega

Matagalpa

El Sauce   PANCASAN

Leon

LAKE MANAGUA

Managua   Tipitapa

Masaya

Granada   LAKE NICARAGUA

Nueva Guinea

SOLENTINAME (Islands)

San Carlos

La Concepción Castle

PACIFIC OCEAN

ATLANTIC OCEAN

COSTA RICA   R. SAN JUAN

CONTENTS

PART 1: CANTO EPICO TO THE FSLN

PART 2: NICARAGUAN VISION AND OTHER POEMS

Sandino (3rd from right) with supporters including his brother Sócrates and Farabundo Martí.

Part 1

CANTO EPICO TO THE FSLN

NICARAGUA NICARAGUITA

Ay Nicaragua, Nicaragüita
la flor más linda de mi querer
abonada con la bendita
Nicaragüita
sangre de Diriangén
Ay Nicaragua sos más dulcita
que la mielita de Tamagás
pero ahora que ya sos libre
Nicaragüita
yo te quiero mucho más.

Frangipani: 'Nicaragüita',
Nicaragua's national flower

The *Canto Epico* begins with a love song to Nicaragua.

NICARAGUA NICARAGUITA

Nicaragua Nicaraguita,[1]
flower of my heart most dear.
That hero and martyr,
Nicaraguita,
died for you: Diriangén.[2]
Nicaragua you are sweeter
than the honey of Tamagás
but now that you're free,
oh Nicaraguita
I love you even more!

SANDINO

En el mero corazón de Las Segovias
donde al jiñocoago
muestra en su piel
el códice de la historia reciente
allí donde el malinche florecido
afila sus machetes en la luna
a sólo dos leguas del Chipote
Sandino
Augusto Calderón Sandino
el hijo natural de sacuanjoche
Sandino
Augusto Calderón Sandino
viene a hablar con los suyos.

On 4th May 1927 Sandino was the only Nicaraguan general to reject the Treaty of Espino Negro, which had been signed by the US envoy Henry Stimson and the Nicaraguan President Moncada. By this treaty Nicaragua agreed to hand over all her arms to the US marines and to the setting up of a Nicaraguan Guard under US supervision and with US officers. Sandino refused to surrender his arms and retreated to the northern mountains of Segovia with a small band of men, women and children, his 'crazy little army'.

SANDINO

In the very heart of the Segovias
where the gumbo limbo[1]
shows in its soft bark
the codex of our recent history
and vermilion flowered the flame tree,[2]
machetes sharpened in the moonlight,
just two leagues from El Chipote,
Sandino
Augusto Calderón[3] Sandino,
natural child of frangipani,[4]
Sandino
Augusto Calderón Sandino
gathered his band and spoke.

EL RAPTO

¿Quién es esa muchacha
que lleva el guerrillero
en el anca segura
de su caballo prieto?
¿Quién es esa chavala
alegre y querendona
como una palomita
como una gongolona?

RESPONDIERON LOS VALLES, LOS RIOS LAS CAÑADAS,
JUNTO A LOS PAJARITOS DE TODA LA MONTAÑA:
ELLA ES LA MAS GALANA, ELLA ES LA MAS BONITA
ELLA ES LA NICARAGUA, LA NICARAGUITA.

¿Quién es esa morena
de pelo suelto al viento
espiga de mozote
pegada al guerrillero?
¿Quién es esa cipota
fragante y transparente
como chorrito de agua
clarita de vertiente?

The guerrilla falls in love with Nicaragua and is 'carried away' to the
dangerous revolutionary struggle in the mountains. Note: she abducts
him!

THE ABDUCTION

Who is this young woman
carrying the guerrilla
safely mounted on her pony
and holding tight behind her?
Who is this young woman,
joyful and loving
like a little pigeon,
like a chinese lantern?[1]

ALL THE VALLEYS ANSWERED, THE RIVERS AND THE GULLIES
AND ALL OVER THE MOUNTAIN THE SMALL BIRDS ADD THEIR VOICES:
NO ONE IS MORE BEAUTIFUL THAN HER, NO ONE IS SWEETER,
SHE IS NICARAGUA, NICARAGUITA.

Who is this dark woman
with wind blowing in her hair,
stuck fast to the guerrilla
like a prickly bur?[2]
Who is this young creature,
sharp-scented and transparent
as the rushing water
in a clear mountain torrent?

Members of Sandino's army 1927 – 1932

8

Sandino with those who accompanied him on his last trip to Managua. From left to right: Sócrates Sandino, Juan Pablo Umanzor, Sandino, Santos López, Francisco Estrada, Juan Ferreti and Salvador Calderón Ramírez.

After the US marines withdrew on 1st January 1933, Sandino and his undefeated army voluntarily laid down their arms. Sandino went four times to Managua for peace talks and on his fourth trip, after a farewell dinner in the Presidential Palace on 21st February 1934, he was murdered by order of the National Guard Chief, Anastasio Somoza García, who shortly afterwards became dictator.

EL NACIMIENTO

Como un chilotito tierno
fulgurante bajo el sol
nace el Frente Sandinista
mazorca y espiga de liberación.
Cada grano fue una bala
para conquistar la paz
y levantamos la milpa
para la tapisca de la libertad.

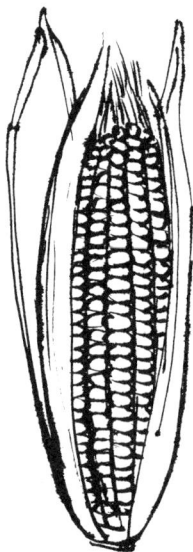

The love affair between Sandino and Nicaragua produces an offspring. On 23rd July 1961, a meeting took place in Tegucigalpa, Honduras between Silvio Mayorga, Carlos Fonseca and Tomás Borge to plan a new revolutionary movement, which came to be called the FSLN: Sandinista National Liberation Front. This date is now the FSLN's official birthday.

THE BIRTH

Like a tender baby corn cob[1]
shining brightly in the sun
sprouted the Sandinista Front
as sweetcorn and spearhead of liberation.
Each grain was a bullet
ready to battle for peace
and we are raising the maize crop
for the harvest home when we'll be free.

LOS ARBOLES

Entonces los venerables patriarcas de la montaña
los árboles, los güegüenses
vinieron por los caminos
a conocer al celeque
a conocer al recién parido.

Desde la tupida cumbre
del Kilambé
la ceiba decidió bajar
milenaria mujer
compañera eterna
del cedro real:
'Implacable en el combate será
generoso en la victoria será.'

Al rato llegó el malinche
del cerro de Ciguatepe
su penacho colorado
insurrección de machetes:
'Serás flor encendida
para los humildes
tajo mortal para los poderosos.'

Del Wisisil
cerro de Metapa
llegó el chilamate frondoso y ladino

At the birth of the FSLN the great trees of Nicaragua are its 'god-mothers' and come to bless the baby. Each tree gives a blessing related to its own nature.

THE TREES

Then all the venerable patriarchs
the trees, the giants of the mountain
took to the roads and set out
to meet the new sprout
to greet the newborn.[1]

From the jungly summit
of Kilambé
descended the silk cotton tree,[2]
age-old woman
eternal companion
of the royal cedar:
'Implacable in combat you'll be,
generous in victory you'll be.'

Soon after that came the flame tree[3]
from the hillside of Ciguatepe
decked out in flamboyant scarlet,
insurrection of machetes:
'*Your flower will flame*
for the humble,
the mighty you'll mortally wound.'

From Wisisil
Metapa mountain
leafy and wise fig laurel[4]

como un profeta de lengua sabia
baila con su tronco retorcido:
'Tronco de cipote, hombre de ñeque
madera de tayacán.'

Y el jocote
el árbol de los amores
vino desde la vertiente
clarita y pura del Ochomogo.
Y el jocote
con sus frutos tronadores
hablantín y zalamero
cundidito de piropos:
'Será un torrente de amor
patentito amor
sin manjunjias ni sontines.'

El espabel con su piel de tambor
va declarando a ritmo de Quijongo:
'Será rojito pizpireto y bravo
como el chile congo
como el chile congo.'

Con su república de pájaros
del mero Coyotepe
el granadillo vino a hablar
roja-amarilla su cotona
viendo al niño se emociona
y se decide a palabrear:
'Sangre dulce y risa de marimba
santo y seña para ser
constructor de la esperanza.'

speaks with its prophetic tongue,
dances with its twisted trunk:
'Child's body, brave man,
hard wood of tayacán.'[5]

And the *jocote*[6]
the hog plum love tree
from beside the Ochomogo's
rushing river comes.
And the *jocote*,
whose fruits bite crackly,
its chatty flattery
loaded with sugar plums:
'You'll be a torrent
of love strong and true
without witchcraft or trickery.'

The cashew[7] with its bark for drum
declares to the Quijongo rhythm:
'You'll be brighter, braver, sharper
than a red hot pepper
than a red hot pepper.'

With its bird republic
from the heart of Coyotepe
rosewood granadillo[8] came to speak.
Its dress was red and yellow
when it saw the little fellow,
it was so excited these words broke:
'Your laugh will ring
sweet as marimba,
signal of hope and constructor.'

Y el legendario jenízaro
güirisero de estrellas y trinos
vino desde Nagarote
y le cantó al cipote
con su voz de siglos:
'Va a ser miel de mariola
para los oprimidos
chichicaste
para los opresores.'

El jícaro no dijo una palabra
y al extender su mano hacia la aurora
diez hojas germinaron en sus ramas
diez puños que escribieron esta historia
diez retoños creciendo en la alborada
diez huellas imborrables, diez semillas
diez perfiles rompiendo la oscurana
cargados de futuro y alegría.

Santos López, one of the ten founders of
the FSLN who had fought with Sandino,
was the newborn Sandinista Front's direct
link with Sandino its 'father'. He died ill
in Havanna in 1965.

And the legendary raintree[9]
miner of tunes and stars
came from Nagarote
to serenade the baby
with its ancient voice:
'For the needy
you'll be mariola honey
but to their oppressors
as a stinging nettle fierce.'

The calabash[10] tree did not say a word
and when it spread its hands out to the morning
ten[11] leaves sprouted on its branches,
ten fists clenched to write this story,
ten shoots of new green in the dawning,
ten prints indelible, ten seeds,
ten faces smiling through the darkness,
bearers of the future and of gladness.

RAITI-BOCAY

Es la primera macoya del Frente
bajo la lluvia feliz
el corazón galopando
bajo sus rotas camisas
como relámpagos van
invadiendo la selva con su sonrisa.

Cada minuto de gesta gloriosa
nacido de nuestra historia
pioneros en los pantanos
pioneros en los naufragios
que se graduaron de hombres
en el aula de la montaña.

Es la primera macoya del Frente:
¡Raití-Bocay!

Un canto de cayucos guerrilleros
el grito secular de los tuneros
la patria en el espejo del Wankí:
¡Raití-Bocay!

From July–October 1963 the FSLN guerrilla force established its base along the Rio Coco on the Honduran border, where their living conditions were appalling. Here and along the River Bocay they clashed with the National Guard. They were able to occupy the villages of Raití and Gualaquistán. There had been guerrilla engagements before but these were the first for the FSLN, with its revolutionary programme. It was the Front's 'first bunch of battles'.

RAITI-BOCAY[1]

This is the *Frente's* first bunch of battles
under the blessing of rain,
their galloping hearts
beneath their torn shirts
like lightning their smiles
invade and flash through the jungle.

Every minute of this glorious action
belongs to our history.
They were pioneers in swamps,
shipwrecked in rivers
and their graduation
was in the school of the mountain.

This is the *Frente's* first bunch of battles
Raití-Bocay!

Canoes full of guerrillas singing,
the rubber tappers' ancient cry[2]
the country in the mirror of Wankí:[3]
Raití-Bocay!

Semilla que cayó en tierra fecunda
génesis de la luz que hoy nos alumbra
la patria en el espejo del Wankí:
¡Raití-Bocay!

Seed which fell on fertile ground,
light struck now shines throughout the land,
the country in the mirror of Wankí:
Raití-Bocay!

PABLO UBEDA

SE DISFRAZA DE ESPADILLO
SE DISFRAZA DE MOZOTE
Y SE CONVIERTE EN POCOYO,
CONEJO, GARROBO, CUSUCO, PISOTE.

Pablo Ubeda pasó
ayer mismo muy temprano,
Carlos Reyna lo encontró
allá en el comisariato.
¿Pero cómo sucedió
que ayer en la madrugada
el juez de mesta lo vio
cruzándose la cañada?
'¿Qué será esta confusión?'
se preguntaba el sargento.
'¿No será que este cabrón
es el mentado cadejo?'
Lo vieron en Kuskawás
en la Tronca y en Waslala.
Ya no lo verán jamás
se lo tragó la montaña.

Pablo Ubeda, whose real name was Rigoberto Cruz, organised clandestine peasant support for the FSLN in the mountains. Carlos Reyna worked with him. Both died at Pancasán on 27th August 1967.

PABLO UBEDA

NOW HE IS DISGUISED AS SWORDGRASS,
NOW HE IS DISGUISED AS SANDBUR[1]
AND HE TURNS INTO A PARROT,
IGUANA, ARMADILLO, COATI, RABBIT!

Pablo Ubeda passed by
yesterday morning early.
Carlos Reyna met him
down at the local store.
So how did it happen
that the same day at dawn
the *mesta*[2] judge saw him
crossing the gully?
'Now what's going on?'
puzzled the sergeant.
'Surely isn't this fellow
the famous *cadejo*?'[3]
They saw him in Kuskawás,
in La Tronca and Waslala.
They won't see him again.
He's been swallowed by the mountain.

Lo ayudan los vientos
las Siete Cabritas
lo oculta el chagüite
lo esconde la milpa.
La guardia dispara
contra el cafetal
y sale Pablito
sereno pajito
bordeando el cañal.

The winds all assist him,
the seven stars shining,
the swamps give him cover
he is hidden by maizefields.
The guard takes a shot
in the coffee plantation
and out strolls Pablito
coolly and neatly
by the sugar cane.

PANCASAN

Cumbre de la cordillera
como un puño de granito
como gigantesco grito: ¡PANCASAN!

Piedra barro arcilla cumbre
roca viva selva y pino
la presencia de Sandino: ¡PANCASAN!

Pleno sol de rebeldía
tras el telón del paisaje
sinfonía del coraje: ¡PANCASAN!

Allí vi a Silvio Mayorga
con granadas y poemas
derribando las estrellas: ¡PANCASAN!

En las aguas coloridas
junto a los tepajonales
Oscar Danilo Rosales: ¡PANCASAN!

Nicolás Sánchez 'El Tigre'
en el Cerro Colorado
como un rojo jiñocuago: ¡PANCASAN!

A guerrilla base was established at Pancasán, about thirty miles east of Matagalpa. On August 27th 1967 Somoza's troops located them and forced them into open combat. The FSLN were defeated and lost thirteen senior members. However this defeat became a political victory, because it gave the FSLN a new political authority throughout Nicaragua as the focus of opposition to the dictator.

PANCASAN[1]

Summit of the range of mountains
like a clenched fistful of granite
like a gigantic single shout: PANCASAN!

Mud and clay and living rock
wooded hillside, pine and stone
and the presence of Sandino: PANCASAN!

High noon sun full-blown rebellion
blazing over all the country
hope and courage symphony: PANCASAN!

There I saw Silvio Mayorga[2]
carrying grenades and poems
bringing down the stars above him: PANCASAN!

In the dark stained waters flowing
through the tangled vegetation
Oscar Danilo Rosales: PANCASAN!

Nicolas Sánchez 'The Tiger'
in the Cerro Colorado
like a mud red gumbo limbo: PANCASAN!

Con el primer fogonazo
fulgurantes sus pupilas
van quemando la neblina: ¡ PANCASAN!

Y Francisco Moreno
el más feliz
cumiche guerrillero
estrena en su cotona de poplín
la rosa de los vientos.
Su risa de chavalo allí no más
salta por los peñascos
y de este carcajada
nace la cascada
limpia de Apanás.

With first powder-flash of battle
brighter still his eyes are flashing
burning through the misty morning: PANCASAN!

And Francisco Moreno,
happy to be
the youngest guerrilla
wears the wind rose
in his poplin shirt.
His boyish laugh
rings across the boulders
and from this laughter
burst the bright waterfall
of Apanás.

CASIMIRO SOTELO

Casimiro Sotelo
amigo camarada
corazón rojinegro
caminante del alba.

Nos prometimos juntos
plantar un mundo nuevo
a partir de este dulce furor
de nuestro sueño.

Te fuiste con el aire
hermano Casimiro
para andar clandestino
por barriadas y montes.

Te vestiste de barro
de limpio barro rojo
para estar en las frescas
tinajitas del pobre.

Casimiro Sotelo was active in the FSLN's essential work of organising inside Nicaragua, in towns, among students and other groups. On 22nd January 1967, 60,000 demonstrated in Managua against Anastasio Somoza Debayle's presidential candidacy and several hundred were massacred by the National Guard. Somoza, predictably elected, introduced a new wave of state terrorism to deal with opposition, especially after Pancasán. During this, on 4th November 1967, Casimiro was captured with three others by the Security Forces in the Managua district of Monseñor Lescano, and assassinated.

CASIMIRO SOTELO

Casimiro Sotelo,
friend and comrade,
black and red hearted
dawnwalker.

We promised together
to make a new world,
that what we had dreamed
with such passion, we'd build.

Into thin air
you disappeared Casimiro
to go clandestine
in city and mountain.

You dressed in mud,
good red mud,
to be like the pots
the poor people had.

Y pienso Casimiro
que vuelas y te encumbras
ávido peregrino
de cantares de gesta.

Con tu pasión erguida
tus sandalias de lluvia
por aulas y caminos
agitando a la gente.

No te imagino ahora
hermano Casimiro
en el espacio frío
devorando galaxias.

Te digo simplemente
hermano Casimiro
corazón rojinegro
caminante del alba.

And I think Casimiro
of you flying high
in heroic song
on your pilgrim way.

With undaunted faith,
wearing rain sandals,
speaking and stirring
you trod roads and halls

I can't imagine you now,
friend Casimiro,
lost in cold space,
that galaxy-devourer.

I simply say:
Casimiro our brother,
black and red hearted
dawnwalker.

JULIO BUITRAGO

En el momento crudo del combate
los héroes no dijeron que morían,
murieron sin decir una palabra
todo el amor cifrado en alegría.
Esa alegría de morir cantando
en Julio fue consigna fulgurante
para construir la patria del mañana
sobre el cimiento rojo de la sangre.

Julio Buitrago was a leader of the urban guerrilla force in Managua and member of the FSLN directorate. On July 15th 1969 his safe house near the Delicias del Volga in the Frixione district of Managua was detected by the Guard and besieged by 400 troops with machine guns and tear gas, backed up by aircraft and a Sherman tank. Five militants were killed including Julio, who held out to the last and died singing the Sandinista Hymn. The dictator had ordered the battle to be televised to inspire terror by showing how he dealt with resistance. The result was the opposite. Julio's heroism became legendary and people began to believe in the FSLN's 'invincibility'.

JULIO BUITRAGO

At the actual moment they were fighting[1]
the heroes did not say that they were dying.[2]
They died without saying a word
all their love turning to joy.
That joy of theirs to die singing
shone out in Julio that day,
building our country tomorrow
on the red foundation of blood.

LEONEL RUGAMA

¿Te acordas de aquel muchacho
el que vendía tortillas
se salió del seminario
pa' meterse a la guerrilla?
Murió como todo un hombre
allá por el cementerio,
cometió el atroz delito
de agarrar la vida en serio.

After leaving the seminary Leonel Rugama joined the urban guerrillas in Managua because he had become convinced that christians should engage in the armed struggle. 'It would be suicide not to.'

He died on 15th January 1970 aged 20, when the National Guard surrounded him and two others in their safe house near the Cementerio Oriental – with lorries, tanks and helicopters.

LEONEL RUGAMA

Do you remember that boy,
the one who sold *tortillas*?
He came out of the seminary
to go and join the guerrillas?
He died every inch a man[1]
down there by the cemetery.
He committed the atrocious crime
of taking life seriously.

LUISA AMANDA ESPINOSA

Como la ropa en las piedras
tu cuerpo quedó tendido
detrás de aquel lavandero
tu blusa de balas tejida.

A mayo se anticipó
y en abril fue tu semilla
dulce y pequeño dolor
sembrada para dar vida.

Luisa Amanda mujer común
pequeña triste y sencilla
tus manos huelen aún
a metralla y a cocina.

Luisa Amanda por fin llamó
a tu puerta la mañana
y la patria hizo mayor
tu corazón de muchacha.

Luisa Amanda Espinosa looked after guerrilla 'nests' in León and ran messages for them. She was shot down by the Guard on 3rd April 1970. 'We saw her for the last time that morning crossing the Calle de Laborio in León. Sweaty, vehement, clutching almost tenderly her bunch of secret papers . . . ' She was the FSLN's first woman militant martyr and has given her name to the Nicaraguan Women's organisation AMNLAE (Luisa Amanda Espinosa Nicaraguan Women's Association).

LUISA AMANDA ESPINOSA

Like clothes spread out to dry
on stones your body lay,
behind that washing place,
your blouse with bullets' embroidery.

May was anticipated,
in April your seed was sown,
in pain your small good
life-giving seed was sown.

Luisa Amanda a common woman,
little and grave and humble.
Even now your hands still smell
of cooking and shrapnel.

Luisa Amanda the morning
finally knocked at your door
and your young girl's heart grew up
when your country summoned.

La cumiche de doña Antonia
la muchacha veintiañera
cuidando nidos viviste
palomita mensajera.

De alero en alero fuiste
palomita mensajera
y en tus manos la esperanza
de campesinas y obreras.

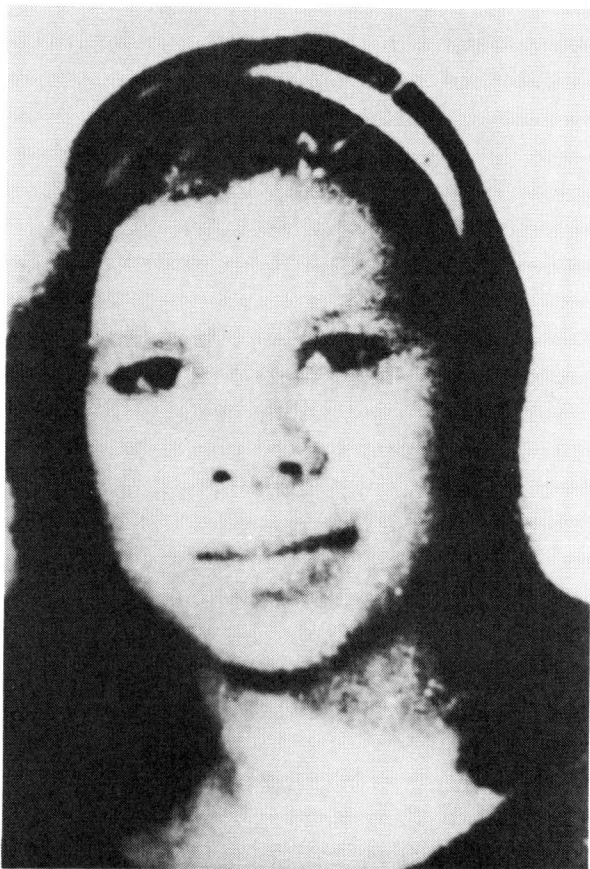

Doña Antonia's youngest,
you were just twenty,
you looked after the nests,
messenger pigeon.

From house to house you flew,
messenger pigeon
carrying the hope with you
of peasant and working women.

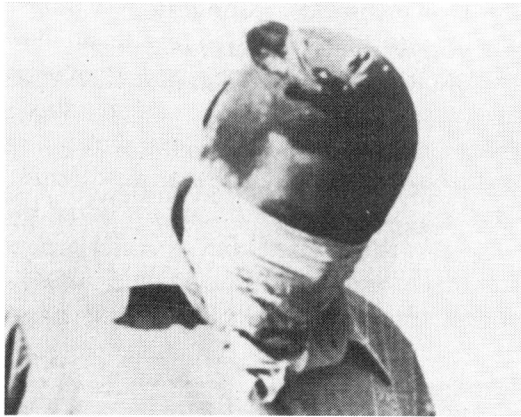

COMANDANTE MARCOS

Infinitas gracias Comandante Marcos
por la arcilla dura que labra tu nombre,
infinitas gracias por la Nicaragua
hecha en la medida de tu sueño enorme.

Infinitas gracias Comandante Marcos
por la primavera que estrena esta patria,
por la savia nueva que viene creciendo
desde las raíces de tu militancia.

Infinitas gracias Eduardo Contreras
comandante hermano, comandante amigo,
comandante escuela, comandante libro,
comandante arado, comandante trigo.

Infinitas gracias Comandante Marcos
por esa estatura de estrella brillante,
por el firme acero de tu frente en alto,
por el río rojo que fluye en tu sangre.

On 27th December 1974 *Comandante* Marcos, who was Eduardo Contreras, led the Juan José Quezada commando raid on Chema Castillo's house in Los Robles, Managua. Chema Castillo was Minister of Agriculture, a rich cotton exporter and close confidant of the dictator. The raid took place during a party for the US Ambassador, Turner B. Shelton. Many important friends of Somoza were at the party and the FSLN held the guests hostage for sixty hours, until its demands were met. These were: the release of 18 political prisoners (including Daniel Ortega and José Benito Escobar), a ransom of two million US dollars and publication of communiques in *La Prensa* and other papers.

Eduardo Contreras died fighting on the Managua-León road on 7th November 1976.

COMANDANTE MARCOS

Infinite thanks *Comandante* Marcos
for the hard clay that moulded your name,
infinite thanks for Nicaragua
made to the measure of your massive dream.

Infinite thanks *Comandante* Marcos
for the spring that has come today to our country,
for the new sap that's starting to rise
from the roots of your militancy.

Infinite thanks Eduardo Contreras,
comandante brother, *comandante* mate,
comandante school, *comandante* book,
comandante plough, *comandante* wheat.

Infinite thanks *Comandante* Marcos
for your shining like a bright star,
for the true steel of your clear forehead,
for the red river that flows in your blood.

Infinitas gracias Comandante Marcos
porque no hubo escollos para tu bravura,
porque el enemigo con su rabia ciega
no pudo a balazos matar tu ternura.

Marcos se detuvo con sus compañeros
bajo la serena paz de un tamarindo.
Le ve un arcoiris terciado en el pecho
la banda celeste de los elegidos.
Desarmó las piezas de su carabina,
con rayos de luna los fue lubricando
pero en vez de balas en los magazines
tenía claveles y lirios del campo.

Infinite thanks *Comandante* Marcos
because you were brave without any fuss,
and the enemy firing in his blind fury
found no force could finish your tenderness.

Marcos stopped with his comrades
under the serene peace of a tamarind tree.
A rainbow lay crosswise over his chest,
sash of the heavenly order of the elect.
He unloaded his rifle
and oiled it with moonbeams
but instead of bullets in the magazines
there were carnations and lilies of the field.

EDGAR MUNGUIA

En el telón de la noche
se lo juro compadrito
vi dos estrellas chachaguas
dos luceros gemelitos.
¿ Serán los ojos brillantes
de un venado lampareado?
¿ Serán tan sólo las luces
del caserío cercano?

Pero allá en Jocote-Tuma
el baqueano Gumersindo
me contestó circunspecto
con su acento campesino:
'Esas luces que en el cielo
parpadean serenitas
son dos luces fulgurantes
patentitas patentitas,
son las pupilas brillantes
de Edgar la Gata Munguía
que nos dicen ¡Adelante!
Ya viene clareando el día.'

Edgar 'La Gata' ('The Cat') Munguía was an FSLN militant, who was one of the leaders of the mass demonstrations and occupations of schools and churches in León in 1971, to obtain the release of political prisoners. He fell in combat at Yaosca near Matagalpa on 13th September 1976.

EDGAR MUNGUIA

On the curtain of the night
truly, my friend, I swear
I saw twin stars,
a brilliant pair.
Are they the gleaming eyes
of a dazzled deer reflected?
Are they just the lights
of the farm over there?

But down in Jocote-Tuma
the guide Gumersindo
answered me circumspectly
in his country accent:
'Those lights in the sky
twinkling serenely
are two flashing beacons
plain to see, plain to see.
They are the shining eyes
of Edgar La Gata Munguía
telling us: Keep going!
Now the day is breaking.'

CARLOS FONSECA

Un ruido de pájaros
predijo tu muerte
y tu sangre dulce
floreció en los malinches
lloró la montaña
y el pájaro león
y el lucero en la aurora
sembró el sudor de tu frente
y creció en Zinica el amor
nuestra liberación
capitán y timón
tayacán de mi pueblo.

Y seguís disparando
con tus ojos azules
emboscando el dolor
sin temor a morir
enseñando a matar
a leer y a escribir
con el Danto y Pedrón
Benjamín Zeledón
con Raudales y Claudia
y Sandino
y los miles de niños caídos
y los miles de muertos
que nunca murieron
como vos.

Carlos Fonseca[1] was one of the original founders of the FSLN and their most revered leader. He was killed at Boca de Piedra in the mountain forest of Zinica on November 8th 1976.

CARLOS FONSECA

An outburst of birds
predicted your death
and your sweet blood
blossomed on the flamboyants,
the mountain wept
and the lion bird,
the morning star
sowed the dew of your forehead
and in Zinica love grew,
our liberation,
captain and helmsman
tayacán of my people.

And you keep on firing,
with your blue eyes
ambushing pain,
not fearing to die,
teaching others to shoot
to read and to write
with El Danto[2], and Pedrón[3],
Benjamin Zeledón[4],
with Raudales[5] and Claudia[6]
and Sandino
and the thousands of fallen children
and the thousands of dead
who never died
like you.

Te mataron cien veces
y cien veces temblaron
los cobardes al verte
nuevo y multiplicado
en Bocay y Zinica
en Raití y Pancasán
en un niño aprendiendo a soñar
un maestro, un obrero un volcán
un puñado de luz
un cuaderno, un arado un fusil
un ejército y pueblo empeñado en parir
una patria madura y feliz
un poder popular.

They killed you a hundred times
and a hundred times cowards
trembled to see you
resurrected redoubled,
in Bocay and Zinica
in Raití and Pancasán,
in a child learning to dream,
a teacher, a worker, volcano,
a fistful of light,
a schoolbook, a rifle, a plough,
an army, whole people set to deliver
a country joyful and ready
to put the people in power.

OCTUBRE

Octubre no es tan sólo referencia
como un mojón que marca nuestra historia.
Octubre es llama traducida en guerra
para prender la cólera del pobre.

Octubre es la lanchita clandestina
con plátanos con mangos con piñas y naranjas
y bajo el tornasol de los jocotes
la guaca cundidita de bombas y granadas.

Octubre floreció en Solentiname
con Elvis, Donald y el Chato Medrano
armados de ternura hasta los dientes
San Carlos despertó para mirarlos.

Octubre es una escuadra de chocoyos
que rompe la quietud del caserío
y se van convirtiendo en guerrilleros
para atacar Mozonte tempranito.

Octubre es La Foquita disparando
con Israel Lewites en Masaya.
Octubre es grito que se va ensanchando
epidemia de luz que nos contagia.

In October 1977 the FSLN launched a new offensive into towns and cities with attacks on the San Carlos Barracks, Mozonte, Masaya and Los Manos.

OCTOBER

October is not just a point of reference,
a landmark that sticks out in our story.
October is a flame roaring into war
because the anger of the poor is catching.

October is the clandestine launching
with bananas and pineapples, oranges and mangoes
and under the hog plums' gleaming shade
the pile is growing higher of bombs and hand grenades.

October flowered in Solentiname
with Elvis, Donald and Chato Medrano,[1]
armed to the teeth with tenderness.
San Carlos awoke that day and saw them.

October is a squadron of parakeets
breaking upon the quiet of the hamlet
and they start turning into guerrillas
to attack Mozonte very early.

October is La Foquita[2] shooting
with Israel Lewites in Masaya.
October is a shout raised and getting louder,
epidemic of light that is contagious.

COMANDANTE FEDERICO

Una lluvia de marimbas, atabales y ocarinas
para pronunciar tu nombre: ¡Comandante Federico!

Un machete en cada verso, un martillo en cada estrofa
para cincelar tu canto: ¡Comandante Federico!

El vuelo azul de un gorrión, todo un pueblo en combustión
para continuar tu huella: ¡Comandante Federico!

Una guitarra en mampuesta bordoneando una epopeya
para cincelar tu gloria: ¡Comandante Federico!

Una bala trazadora disparada hacia la aurora
para resumir tu gesta: ¡Comandante Federico!

Comandante Federico was Pedro Arauz[1]. He fell fighting in an important ambush of the National Guard on the Masaya–Tipitapa road on 17th October 1977.

COMANDANTE FEDERICO

A shower of marimbas, ocarinas, kettle drums,
to utter your name: *Comandante* Federico!

A machete in every line, a hammer in every verse
to engrave your praise: *Comandante* Federico!

A sparrow's blue flight, the whole country alight
to follow in your footsteps: *Comandante* Federico!

A guitar in hand strumming an epic story
to sing out your glory: *Comandante* Federico!

A tracer bullet fired into the dawn
to describe your action: *Comandante* Federico!

CAMILO ORTEGA

Sonaron los atabales
tremolaron las marimbas
todos los alcarabanes
repitieron la consigna.
Empuñando la bandera
roja y negra sandinista
Camilo Ortega Saavedra
hacia la aurora marchó.

Tu sangre pura Camilo
va creciendo en las pitahayas
en la risa de los niños
de mi amada Nicaragua.
Tu sangre pura Camilo
llamarada en la montaña
derramó sobre mi patria
su violenta floración.

Camilo Ortega was the younger brother of Daniel (now President) and Humberto Ortega (now Minister of Defence). He led the FSLN's Internal Front to take the city of Granada in February 1978. Shortly afterwards he was sent by the FSLN to give support and leadership to the spontaneous uprising in Monimbó, an Indian district of Masaya. Monimbó was held for a week from 20th February 1978. Camilo was killed on 26th February in Las Sabogales, Masaya.

CAMILO ORTEGA

The kettle drums rumbled,
the marimbas trembled
and all the stone curlews
repeated the order.
Grasping the black and red
Sandinista banner
Camilo Ortega Saavedra
marched off towards morning.

Your true blood Camilo
bears fruit on the pitahayas,[1]
and the children's laughter
in my beloved Nicaragua.
Your true blood Camilo,
fire on the mountain,
has spread over my country
its violent flowering.

JOSE BENITO ESCOBAR

Usted compañero
es de los de siempre
de los quijotes,
los incurables tercos,
de los amancebados
a plena luz del día
con el rabioso sueño
de los justos.

Por eso justamente
no lo olvida el obrero
y su nombre gravita
entre las asembleas,
por su actitud honrada,
serena sin dobleces,
por esa resistencia
de mole sensitiva,
por su fe de montaña
más heroica y bravía
que todos los golgotas unidos
de la tierra.

José Benito Escobar was a member of the FSLN's National Directorate. Born of working class parents in Managua in 1936, he was an activist in the construction workers' strike of 1958 and in 1960 he co-founded the JRN (Nicaraguan Revolutionary Youth). He was assassinated by the National Guard in Estelí on July 16th 1978.

JOSE BENITO ESCOBAR

You *compañero*
are one of the everlastingly
Quixotic,
the incurably stubborn,
one of those dedicated
to the bright light of day
with the just man's furiously
unswerving vision.

That is why rightly
the workers don't forget you
and your name is spoken
in the assemblies,
because you were honest,
calm and straightforward,
because you resisted
like a feeling rock,
your faith was a mountain
and your bravery more heroic
than all the calvaries
of this earth in one.

EL ASALTO AL PALACIO

Veintidós de agosto del setentiocho
en este corrido se los cuento yo
noticias llegadas desde Nicaragua
cuentan que en Managua la cosa empezó.

Veinticinco compas con los uniformes
de los genocidas de Tacho el Chigüin
entraron muy serios al mero palacio
donde sesionaba el Congreso feliz.

Ya los diputados y los senadores
estaban metidos en plena infanzón
manteniendo al filo de leyes funestas
un brutal sistema de ruin opresión.

El tremendo susto de los congresales
cuando la metralla furiosa bramó
y ese mismo día la ciudadanía
por primera vez la verdad sesionó.

On 22nd August 1978 the Rigoberto Lopez Perez commando conducted the 'Operation Death to Somoza: Carlos Fonseca Amador' and entered the National Palace disguised in National Guard uniforms.[1]

They held the deputies hostage for 47 hours, after which Somoza was forced to agree to their demands. The chief of these was the release of eighty-five political prisoners. The fifty-eight who were still alive were released and flew to Panama in a plane provided by the Panama government. Huge crowds turned out to cheer them all the way to the airport.

THE ASSAULT ON THE PALACE

On the twenty-second of August 1978
I'll tell you the story, this is my song,
the news came out to us from Nicaragua[2]
they say that in Managua it all began.

Twenty-five comrades wearing the uniforms
of the genocidal troops of Tacho the Kid[3]
solemnly entered the National Palace
where without a care the Congress did sit.

And all the deputies, and all the senators
were having a whale of a time, a ball,
maintaining a system of vicious oppression
by a succession of murderous laws.

The awful fright of the members of congress
when the furious thunder of gunfire roared out,
spoke that very day for the citizenry
and for the first time there truth took its seat.

Algunos ingenuos no entendían mucho
pero se quitaron la duda allí no más
cuando un rojinegro pañuelo en el cuello
les hablaba claro de la identidad.

Allí estaban todos temblando de miedo
Luis Pallais Debayle y Panchito Argeñal
todos preocupados rezando el rosario
porque son los cómplices del caporal.

Dicen que Somoza pegó un brinco padre
cuando le contaron todito el pastel
igualito a un león encerrado en su jaula
fumaba y fumaba sin saber que hacer.

Cuarenta y siete horas de espera angustiosa
veinticinco compas prestos a morir
si Tacho no acepta los puntos del Frente
los peces más gordos se truenan allí.

Pasados dos días del operativo
en este corrido se los cuento yo
Somoza se daba contra las paredes
y contra su gusto el negocio aceptó.

De la celda oscura salieron los presos
adelante de ellos camina Tomás
con la decisión de seguir el proceso
siempre hacia adelante sin ver para atrás.

Bájate del nido cantor zanatillo
repite conmigo este hermoso cantar:
!Qué viva la patria de Augusto Sandino
que marcha seguro a la recta final!

Some simple souls were quite bewildered
but shortly they were relieved of all doubt
when a black and red scarf round the neck of a comrade
told them quite plainly what these folk were at.

So they all sat there quaking with fear
Luis Pallais Debayle and Panchito Argeñal[4]
all in a tizzy and saying the rosary
for they were accomplices, Corporal's men.

They say that Somoza leapt up to the ceiling
when he was given the account of all this,
paced like a lion locked up in his cage,
smoking and smoking and quite at a loss.

Forty-seven hours passed anxiously waiting
twenty-five comrades ready to die.
If Tacho won't accept the demands of the *Frente*
the biggest fish here will have had it today.

After two days of this operation,
this is the story my song has to tell:
Somoza was cornered and he had no option,
agreed to the bargain against all his will.

From their dark cells out came the prisoners,
striding in front of them see Tomás[5] walk,
firmly decided to go on with the process
keep going forward and never look back.

Come down from your nest and sing little grackle,[6]
sing out with me this beautiful tale:
Long live the country of Augusto Sandino
faithfully marching to its final goal!

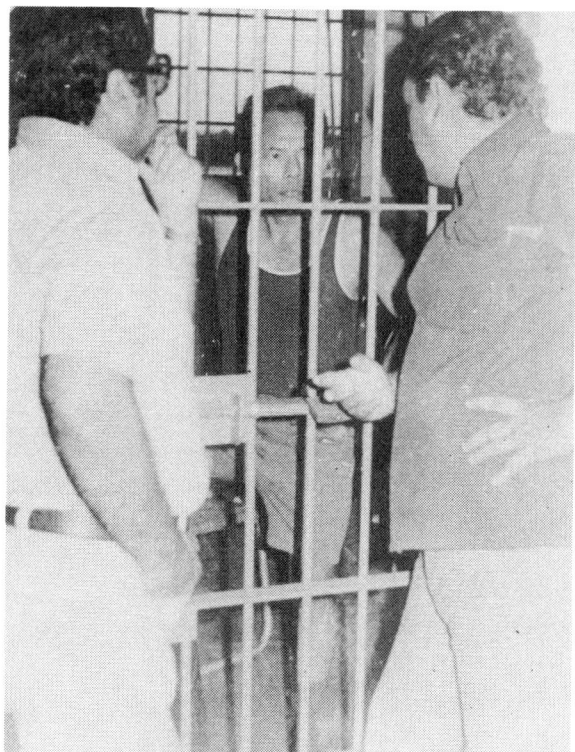

Tomás Borge in
prison and in the
bus carrying
liberated prisoners
to the airport.

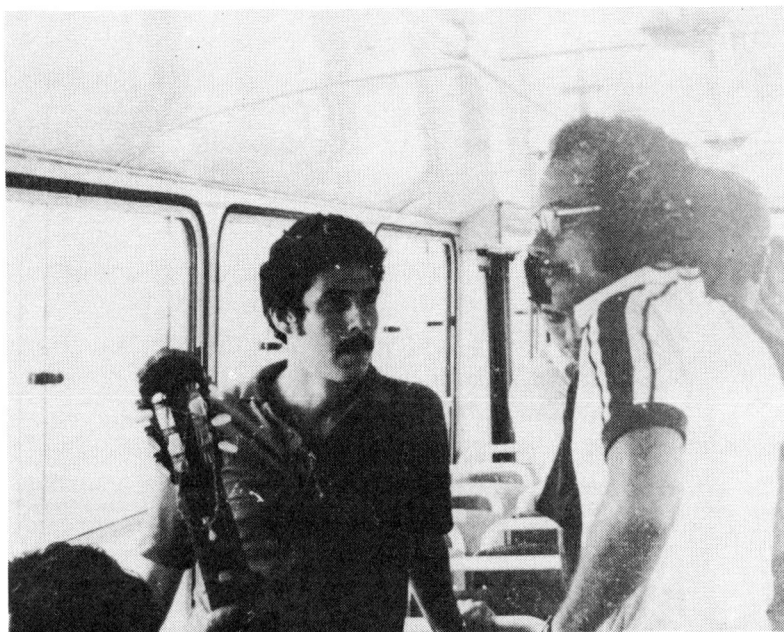

Other prisoners liberated by the Assault on the Palace.

MATAGALPA

El gallo rompió la bruma entre los pinares,
su canto fue trazadora en la madrugada,
se alzó un vuelo de pocoyos trasnochadores
y los güises y zanates
se tomaron los traspatios,
las calles y los zaguanes de Matagalpa.

Hay una mano golpeando de puerta en puerta,
es la patria que nos llama a la insurreccción
y en el umbral del Guanuca
a·boquejarro el paisaje
desemvainó su coraje el Septentrión.

Como la orquídea que sube entre los barrancos,
Crescencio Rosales llama a la juventud
y en sus cajitas de pino
los correos clandestinos
van repartiendo puñitos de nueva luz.

En El Tule una viejita madrugadora
aliña su burusquita para el fogón
y apareció el guerrillero,
lucero nixtayolero,
inaugurando septiembre con su canción.

After the Assault on the Palace, even before the FSLN gave the signal, the people of the northern town of Matagalpa came out on strike and rose in insurrection. By 27th August the districts of El Chorizo and La Chispa were in their hands. The strike continued and on 9th September the FSLN gave the call for insurrection throughout the country.

MATAGALPA

The cock cracked through the mist among the pine trees,
it crowed a tracer bullet into daybreak,
up flocked the parrot night-revellers
and the kiskadees and grackles
took over the backyards,
the alleyways and streets of Matagalpa.

From door to door a raised arm passes knocking,
summoning us to insurrection now!
And where the Guanuca[1] lies
and the landscape hits your eyes,
the North took up its courage, showing how.

Like an orchid growing up in the deep valleys,
Crescencio Rosales calls the young to fight
and in little pinewood boxes
the clandestine post workers
deliver and spread fistfuls of new light.

In El Tule[2] an old woman rising early
prepared a bit of kindling for her stove
and suddenly the guerrilla,
nixtayol[3] morning star,
stood there in song to start September off!

ESTELI

Yo soy la mera cascada de La Estanzuela
a sólo veinte minutos del Tomabú,
soy hija de un ojo-de-agua y una vertiente
soy nieta del gran patriarca el cerro Quiabú.

Yo tengo mi novio allá por la montañita,
le llaman por estos valles el Estelí.
¡Hay que verlo pizpireto cada domingo
con su cotona de manta y calzón de dril!

¡Estelí! Implacable guerrillero
indomable dulce y fiero
combatiente del amor.
¡Estelí! De los cerros aledaños
baja Dávila Bolaños
a cantar tu insurrección.

¡Estelí! Una columna de pinos
descendió por los caminos
en perfecta formación
y al llegar bajo el cielo segoviano
como heroicos milicianos
se cuadraron ante vos.

In September 1978 after Matagalpa, Estelí rose in insurrection and again in April 1979.

ESTELI

I am the waterfall of Estanzuela
only twenty minutes from Tomabú,
daughter of a mountain spring and river,
granddaughter of the great Hill Patriarch Quiabú.

My lover is up yonder in the mountain,
in these valleys they call him Estelí.
You should just see him every Sunday
in his cotton shirt and denims dressed to kill!

Estelí! Implacable guerrilla,
ferocious sweet and fearless
warrior of love.
Estelí! To sing your insurrection
down came Davila Bolaños[1]
from the hills above.

Estelí! A column of pine trees
marched down the road
in perfect formation.[2]
When they reached you they halted,
like brave soldiers they saluted
and stood to attention.

EL CASTILLO DE LA CONCEPCION

Soy el Castillo de la Concepción
y tengo tantas cosas que contar
muchos siglos cabalgan en mi voz
empapada en la espuma del San Juan.

Aún guardo en mis silentes atalayas
el eco austero de lejanos días
cuando una Rafaela iluminada
hundió a la pertinaz piratería.

Pero esta vez pretende mi garganta
de la reciente hazaña hacer memoria
y vengo a relatarles una gesta
que ya es parte vital de nuestra historia.

La Concepción Castle stands on the River San Juan, which forms part of the frontier with Costa Rica. Here the Castle tells the story of the Nueva Guinea Front, in this extreme south-eastern region of Nicaragua.

On May 17th 1979 the Jacinto Hernandez column crossed the Costa Rican border at Los Sabalos, near La Concepción. The plan was to infiltrate the region and mount guerrilla attacks, which would divert National Guard forces from the cities. They succeeded in diverting massive Somozan forces to the area but they were detected and almost the whole 126-strong column wiped out in open country.

LA CONCEPCION CASTLE

I am the Castle of La Concepción
and I can tell so many tales,
many centuries parading in my voice
drenched with San Juan's spray against my walls.

In my silent watch towers I still hold
the austere echo of that far off day
when enlightened Rafaela[1] wrecked
those pirates who refused to go away.

But this time what it is I want to do
is call a recent deed to memory
and I am going to tell you of an action
that's vital part now of our history.

Hacia la plenitud del horizonte
yo los miré salir muy de mañana
con sus mochilas llenas de canciones
repletas de fervor y madrugada.

Partía el Comandante Montenegro
con los enamorados de la patria
con ciento veintiséis hombres enteros
con ciento veintiséis sonrisas claras.

Al mirar tanto amor en esos ojos
constelados, felices y resueltos
le platiqué al San Juan si fuera joven
yo me iría a pelear con todos ellos.

Y sin decir palabra en ese instante
el raudal se alistó bien tempranito
se fue a Nueva Guinea clandestino
en el pelo entrecano de Domingo.

Los vi en el chacalín los vi en el lirio,
los vi llegar al paso de las yeguas.
Allí el dolor me ladra en los sentidos
y me duele la historia en cada piedra.

Hoy se derrama el sol de la victoria
bañando Mancarrón y la Cigüeña,
en ese botecito de la historia
canaleteando va Felipe Peña.

Comandante Rosendo esta alegría
es fruto sazonado por tu sangre.
Comandante Rosendo ya es de día
mañana seguiremos informando.

Over there towards the far horizon
I watched them leave together very early
with their kitbags bursting full of songs,
crammed with daybreak and intensity.

Out set Comandante Montenegro[2]
with those who were in love with their country,
a hundred and twenty six brave souls,
a hundred and twenty six bright smiles.

When I saw such love shining in their eyes,
so determined, so starry and so joyful,
I told San Juan if I was young
I'd go off and fight with them as well.[3]

And without saying a word
the old river enlisted in the small hours,
he went clandestine to Nueva Guinea
wearing Domingo's greying hairs.

I saw them in the shrimp and in the lily,
at a brisk trot I saw them arriving.
There all my senses are shot through with pain,
history hurts me there in every stone.

Today now shines the sun of victory
bathing Mancarrón and La Cigüeña.[4]
In that little boat of history
paddling along there goes Felipe Peña.[5]

Comandante Rosendo[6] this great joy
is a fruit seasoned by your blood.
Comandante Rosendo now it's day,
tomorrow we'll be keeping you informed.

EL DANTO

Cantaba el pájaro león:
'¡yo lo vide, yo lo vide!'
emboscando al agresor,
al tigre de verde olivo.

La ceiba y el cedro real
daban sombra, daban nido
y el ocote y frute-pan
alimento y pan al indio.

Debajo de lo nacido
de su árbol legendario
un chilincoco dulcito
era el corazón del Danto.

En su piel dura el dolor
repicaba convocando
a la unidad y al amor
Germán Pomares llamando.

El Danto (The Tapir) was Germán Pomares Ordoñez. He was a peasant who became a member of staff of the Northern Front. When he joined he could not read but he learnt in the FSLN. It was his famous saying 'and also teach them to read', which became the motto of the post-Revolutionary highly successful literacy campaign.

On 27th March 1979 he led eighty guerrillas[1] to occupy El Jicaro. This was the first step in the general insurrectional plan drawn up by the FSLN's newly formed single National Directorate. He died of wounds on May 24th 1979 leading the attack on Jinotega.

EL DANTO: THE TAPIR

The lion bird sang:[2]
'yes I seen him, yes I seen him!'
ambushing the attacker,
the olive green tiger.

Silk cotton and royal cedar
gave nest, gave shade
and torch pine and bread fruit
were the Indian's fuel and food.

Beneath its shell grown
on its legendary tree,
El Danto's heart
was a sweet coconut.

On his tough skin
pain knocked to summon:
Be united, love one another,
Germán Pomares calling.

Un veinticuatro de mayo
su pecho se estremeció
y la tierra segoviana
su sangre dulce empapó.

El Danto con su mirada
prendió nuestra cordillera
y los ríos arrastraron
el fuego de sus arterias.

De la espiga de su puño
implacable, dulce y violento
la nueva milpa nació
y la cólera del pueblo.

Y ahora que las madrugadas
de julio son diferentes
es que en toda nuestra patria
¡Viejo Pancho estás presente!

On the twenty fourth of May
his breast exploded
and the soil of Segovia
soaked up his blood.

His steady gaze
held fast our mountains
and down all our rivers
swept the fire in his veins.

His fist clasped a blade
of implacable courage,
the new maize sprouting,
the people's rage.

And now that mornings in July
are altogether different,
it's because all through our country
Old Pancho you are present!

LA HUELGA

Unámonos, unámonos, unámonos, unámonos,
juntemos brazos para dar el golpe,
juntemos fuerzas para alzar la voz,
seamos todos como un hormiguero,
juntemos todos ponzoña y ponzoña,
juntemos todos dolor con dolor,
un granito de arena, otro grano de arena,
y otro y otro y otro,
una llama se enciende, otra llama responde,
encendamos la noche,
pongamos el llano en llamas,
pongamos el llanto en llamas,
pongamos la noche en llamas
¡y por güevo tiene que amanecer!

On 31st May 1979 the FSLN called for a general strike: 'Heroic people of Nicaragua, the hour for the overthrow of the dictatorship has come . . .' This message was signed by all three FSLN tendencies from 'somewhere in Nicaragua' and broadcast on Radio Sandino. The strike began on 4th June 1979 and was massively supported.

THE STRIKE

Join together, join together, join together, join together,
join arms to strike the blow,
join lungpower to raise our voice,
let's all be like an ant heap,
all adding poison to poison,
all piling pain upon pain,
one grain of sand, one more grain of sand
and another, another, another,
one flame is lit, another flame answers,
set fire to the night
let's set the country on fire,
let's set the crying on fire,
let's set the darkness on fire
and damn it, dawn has got to break!

LA CATEDRAL DE LEON

Yo que guardo celosa en mis entrañas
las cenizas ilustres de Darío
he visto transitar ante mis ojos
la gloria y el esplendor, el poderío.

Yo miré el río de la sangre dulce
el veintitrés de julio memorable
mientras la rancia aristocracia indiferente
en sus sueños de mimbre deliraba.

Aquella noche de septiembre
yo miré a Rigoberto
iba caminando sin vacilaciones
hacia la cita exacta con la historia.

Con estos cuatro siglos a mi espalda
abandoné mi rol de monumento,
desperté de la gloria y el letargo,
me hice miliciana combatiente.

In the Final Offensive León, Nicaragua's second largest city and ancient stronghold of Somoza's Liberal Party, was the centre for the North Western Rigoberto Lopez Perez Front. On 2nd June 1979 the FSLN entered León, on 17th June the National Guard barracks fell and on 20th June a local revolutionary Junta was set up there. On 9th July León was declared liberated. Finally, as soon as Somoza fled the country on 17th July, the FSLN transferred the Government Junta of National Reconstruction, which it had set up in Costa Rica, to León. This is why at the end of the song all the Cathedral's bells start ringing.

LEON CATHEDRAL

I who closely guard inside me
the illustrious ashes of Darío[1]
have seen splendour, power and glory
passing here before my eyes.

I saw their sweet blood flowing like a river
that memorable July the Twenty Third[2]
while the indifferent aristocracy
rocked their fevered dreams and never cared.

That September night
I watched Rigoberto[3]
walking with no hesitation
to keep his exact appointment with history.

With these four centuries upon my shoulders
I stopped being just a monument,
I awoke from my historic lethargy,
joined up and became a militant.

Porque en mis torres se negó la piedra
a ser la pieza amorfa del pasado
y cada torre se volvió trinchera
para fortificar a los muchachos.

De La 21 huyeron los sicarios
al último reducto de Acosasco,
herido el capataz y cancerbero
los peones de la muerte han claudicado.

Lupe Moreno ataca de sorpresa,
el enemigo tiembla en San Felipe,
como un mancebo bíblico en la guerra
Abel va ajusticiando a los Caínes.

El nombre de Araceli Pérez Darias
irrumpe en la parábola de un grito,
su espíritu se crece en la batalla
como un madroño erguido al infinito.

Julio explotó con fusiles y canciones
y las casonas coloniales se tupieron
de rojinegras banderas y palomas
y golondrinas milicianas florecieron
en mis aleros contagiados de victoria.

In my towers the very stones refused
to be dumb blocks of the past and uninvolved,
every nook and cranny did for trenches
and fortified defences for the lads.

From the Twenty-One[4] the hired assassins fled
to the last redoubt of Acosasco,[5]
torturer and warden now are wounded,
death's menials have given up their job.

Lupe Moreno[6] attacking by surprise,
the enemy trembles there in San Felipe.
Abel now is executing Cain,
the bible story turned the other way.

The name of Araceli Pérez Darias
is hurled in the parabola of a shout.
Like a spring lily growing ever taller
in the battle greatly grows her spirit.

July was full of guns and songs,
black and red flags and doves
decked the great colonial houses
and militant swallows in droves
thronged my rafters infected with victory.

EL REPLIEGUE

No había que pisar ramas
ni hacer ruido con hojas secas,
y la orden fue cumplida
hasta por la naturaleza.

No se oían las chicharras
ni los chayules ni los ronrones,
sólo se oía el latido
de todos los corazones.

Queriendo alcanzar Masaya,
queriendo entrar a Masaya,
aquella columna de agua
de sudor y de esperanza.

Milicianos combatientes
bajo la noche cerrada,
mujeres, niños y viejos
curtidos por la batalla.

Divisamos Nindirí
territorio liberado
pero la orden del Frente
fue cumplida palmo a palmo.

On 27th June 1979 after holding the eastern sector of Managua the capital for nineteen days, the FSLN ordered a strategic retreat to Masaya to the south east. Six thousand people left Managua secretly that night in single file. The tactic was successful and within a month the regrouped revolutionary forces re-entered Managua in triumph.

THE RETREAT

We were not to tread on branches
or allow dry leaves to crackle
and the order was carried out
even by nature as well.

There was not a squeak from the cicadas
or mosquitoes, no insects buzzing,
the only sound to be heard was
the thud of all those hearts thumping.

Wanting to get to Masaya,
wanting to enter Masaya,
we were a column of hope
and drenching sweat and water.

Militant combatants,
bold midnight veterans,
women, children, old people,
all toughened by the battle.

We caught sight of Nindirí,[1]
liberated territory
but the *Frente's* order
was obeyed to the last degree.

Mantuvimos la cautela
para no ser detectados,
con su aliento de coraje
nos animaba el Santiago.

So as not to be detected
cautious how we go,
and with his breath of courage
cheered on by Santiago.[2]

EL TRIUNFO

A veinte años de lucha inclaudicable
juramos defender nuestra victoria,
cada gota de sangre guerrillera,
cada bala y cada vida rojinegra.

No habrá fuerza, ni técnica ni humana,
capaz de detener a un pueblo armado,
los campesinos los obreros estudiantes milicianos
¡Defenderemos la Revolución!

De norte a sur, de mar a mar
no habrá rincón de nuestra patria sin cuidar
en el ingenio, el cafetal
en los cortes de algodón y el arrozal.

Siempre será diecinueve,
siempre será veintitrés,
siempre será julio heroico
avanzando siempre sin retroceder.

Ellos sembraron el sol,
ellos sembraron amor,
y hoy nosotros defendemos la vida,
la cosecha encendida
¡La Revolución!

On 17th July Somoza fled to Miami and in the small hours of 19th July the National Guard finally collapsed in Managua. Radio Sandino woke the nation with a proclamation of victory, well known songs (!) and the Sandinista hymn. It broadcast the first instructions of the new Government ordering discipline and generosity to the defeated enemy. From all parts of the country, thousands of FSLN troops poured into Managua and red and black flags appeared everywhere.

THE TRIUMPH

After twenty years of struggle day by day,
we swear to defend our victory,
every drop of blood guerrillas shed,
every bullet, every life that's black and red.

There'll be no force, technical or human,
that can hold back the people who have risen,
peasants workers students militants in arms
we'll all defend the Revolution!

From north to south, from sea to sea
we'll take care in every corner of our country
in coffee field and cotton cutting,
in rice field and factory.

It will always be the Nineteenth.
It will always be the Twenty Third. [1]
It will always be heroic July
with no retreat, just going forward.

They sowed the sun,
they sowed love
and we today are defending our lives,
our harvest home
and our Revolution!

The FSLN enter Managua.

Carlos Fonseca

Part 2

NICARAGUAN VISION
AND OTHER
POEMS

OPTICA NICARAGÜENSE

'En ese instante apareció Carlos Fonseca. Llegó hasta nosotros con sus ojos bruscos, miopes y azules . . . Carlos murió con el fusil en la mano, con el corazón desbordado de amor hacia los hombres, con los ojos azules apuntando hacia el futuro.'

TOMAS BORGE

Nicaragüense, quien quiera que seas,
sin distingo de pelo, color ni tamaño:
¿Ya se midió usted la vista? ¿No es usted corto de visión?
¿Diferencia bien el azul del rojo, la A de la B y de la C?
¿No padece a pleno sol de cegueras nocturnas?
No descuide sus ojos, son los únicos que tiene
para asomar a un hombre luminoso u oscuro.
Y aunque los tenga formidables,
yo le aconsejo que visite y le quite
de inmediato sus gafas a Carlos Fonseca,
amador de oficio y no oculista.

Aún más: métase en sus pupilas azules
que dicen que eran miopes;
pero que traspasaron la luz del día presente
como si fueran la luz misma de la misma,
porque no todo lo que se ve se siente
porque no todo lo que está a la vista está a la vista
y necesitamos con urgencia de sus lentes, de sus ojos.
Sus ojos precisan la mira,
sus lentes son de contacto.

Por eso tu mirada se hará
una sola, continua caricia
y donde la pongas,
colocarás la bala o la vida.

NICARAGUAN VISION

'At that moment Carlos Fonseca appeared. He came up to us with his staring, short-sighted blue eyes ... Carlos died with his gun in his hand, his heart overflowing with love for humanity and his blue eyes pointing towards the future.'

TOMAS BORGE

Nicaraguan, whoever you are,
whatever your size, the colour of your skin or hair,
have you tested your eyes, are you short-sighted,
can you tell blue from red, A from B from C?
Do you suffer from night blindness in strong sun?
Take care of your eyes, they are the only ones you've got
to discern a person, light or dark.
And even if your eyes are very good,
I advise you to visit Carlos Fonseca
and get his glasses straight away.
He was no optician but a lover[1] of his work.

Further: put yourself in his own blue ones,
which they say were myopic
but pierced the light of the present day
as if they were its very light of light,
because not everything that's seen is felt,
not everything in sight is in sight
and we urgently need his lenses, his eyes.
His eyes focus our looking
and his lenses are contact lenses.

Thus your gaze will turn
into a single continuous caress
and where you direct it
you will put your bullet or your life.

Ver será entonces tanto como oír,
gustar, oler, tocar
y ver de nuevo, amar
y amar es el único sentido
que es todos.

Con esos sus lentes se ve clarísimo el verde verde aquel
de las montañas del norte
que da ganas de ser caballo,
el almacén de la sabandija,
el lago que somete en su entraña
el ademán de pájaro que tiene el cielo,
la vegetal efervescencia del volcán que es la turba
turbia y salada como la brisa de la esperanza.
Verás que Sandino no es un hombre, sino una vereda,
un camino con el zacate sollamado
y las chicharras ordenando silencio:
'Allí va un pueblo clandestino.'
Nicaragüense, paisano inevitable, quien quiera que seas,
busca esos lentes, métete en los ojos de Carlos Fonseca.
Todavía hay tiempo. Recordá que el hombre
nunca se permitió cerrar los ojos ni siquiera ya muerto.

Then seeing will be like hearing,
tasting, smelling, touching
and seeing anew: loving.
For loving is the only sense
that is all the senses.

With his lenses you can see clearly
that green green of the northern mountains
that makes you want to be a horse,
the store which is an insect heap,
the lake whose depths contain
the bird's trajectory in the sky
and the volcano's vegetal effervescence, turf
thick and salty as the breeze of hope.
You will see that now Sandino
isn't a man but a road, a path with scorched grass
and the cicadas ordering silence:
'There a people go clandestine.'
Whoever you are, my fellow Nicaraguan,
get those lenses, Carlos Fonseca's eyes.
There is still time. Remember this was a man
who kept his eyes open even when he was dead.

EPITAFIO DE LOS 50 MIL

Viajero: aquí yacemos 50 mil hombres,
hacia donde pongas los ojos o vuelvas el rostro
encontrarás cruces, estelas, lápidas
con alguna foto nuestra, fechas, nombres
coreados con lástima, furia y orgullo.

Cada quien viviendo su caída o muerte
en épocas distintas, flancos, trincheras y frentes,
sorprendidos acaso del amor, del valor o del miedo
que nos hizo mártires y héroes.
Oyenos clamar,
escucha cómo al rumor de 50 mil voces
asciende una Nicaragua iluminada.

Sandinista combatants during the Final Offensive.

EPITAPH FOR THE FIFTY THOUSAND[1]

Traveller: here we lie, fifty thousand of us.
Wherever you turn, or rest your eyes
you will find crosses, stones, memorials
with photos of us, dates and names
that each in sorrow, rage and pride proclaims.

Each keeping alive a death or fall in combat
at different times, trenches, flanks, fronts,
astonished perhaps at the love, courage or fear
that made heroes and martyrs of us.
Hear our shout,
listen how the sound of 50,000 voices
raises a Nicaragua shining bright.

JORGE NAVARRO

Digan de mí, de Jorge Navarro
Navarrito-Terrabona, muerto en Bocay
Jorge-Cebolla toca-guitarra y acordeón
en cuartos y pensiones universitarias,
que más que fundador y tesorero del FSLN
fui fundador de su alegría.

JORGE NAVARRO

Let them say of me, Jorge Navarro
Navarrito-Terrabona, who died at Bocay,[1]
Jorge the Onion, guitar and accordion
player in university rooms and lodgings,
that as well as being a founder
of the FSLN and its treasurer,
I founded its joy.

SILVIO MAYORGA

Junto a Carlos y Tomás
en desgraciadas cafeterías de Costa Rica,
en Caracas o Cuba organizando
'Juventud Revolucionaria Nicaragüense',
entre quiebres y heridas en Sang Sang,
a través de lepras y tifoideas de montaña,
desde Patuca hasta mi muerte en combate:
Pancasán de 1967,
siempre tuve la secreta certeza del triunfo.
El triunfo brilló para mí distante tal vez
lejano acaso, pero fijo y límpido
como aquel lucero que sobre el ancho y oscuro Río Coco
ascendía la tarde.

SILVIO MAYORGA[1]

Together with Carlos and Tomás
in scruffy Costa Rican cafes,
in Cuba or Caracas organising
'Nicaraguan Revolutionary Youth',
broken bones and wounds in Sang Sang,
leprosy and typhoid in the mountain,
from Patuca till my death in combat:
1967 at Pancasán,
I was always secretly certain that we'd win.
The triumph shone for me,
far off maybe in the distance
but clear and steadfast as the star that rose
over the broad dark Río Coco
in the evening.

ESTELA POR JULIO BUITRAGO

El más joven de los guerreros:
moreno y delgado, a quien hicieron
orinar la sangre, pero no dijo nada en la OSN.
Todo él y él solo fue la resistencia urbana.
Ejército del pueblo, bello y terrible, formado en batalla.

Y si no que lo digan
400 efectivos de la GN derrotados;
los Sherman y Garand, las Browning en reculada
allá por el barrio Frixione;
las colonias, repartos y avenidas llenas de buses
y taxis de la vieja Managua, convertidas
en manigua, crique, montaña.

MONUMENT FOR JULIO BUITRAGO[1]

Youngest of warriors, dark and thin.
They made him piss blood
but he said nothing in the OSN.[2]
He on his own was wholly the urban resistance.
Beautiful and terrible, people's army,
burnished in battle.

And if you don't believe it,
ask the 400 defeated National Guardsmen,
the Shermans, Garands and Brownings[3] in retreat
in the district of Frixione;
every area, every part
of old Managua, all the avenues
packed with buses, taxis, changed
to jungle, creek and mountain.

LEONEL RUGAMA
1949-1970

Aquí yazgo yo, Leonel Rugama Rugama,
dos veces Rugama y apenas mayor de edad
(y esto que dicen que 20 años no es nada).
Yo que amé los circos de pueblo
con las carpas desguasadas o llenas de remiendos,
azotadas como balandros por los vientos de enero.
Hijo de una cándida maestra de escuela
y de Pastor Rugama, el carpintero,
buen viejo barrigón, oloroso
al cedro aserrado en la tarde,
a quien mi alma hecha bala pasó
refilándole una de las piernas
en la insurección de septiembre.

Yo que me afané en buscar un rostro,
acaso el de Ella en las ventanillas
de todos los taxis y buses raudos y urbanos,
para jamás verla ni encontrarla,
sino hasta el último momento.
Cuando se agotó el parque
y halé el gatillo
la tuve cara a cara, frente a frente
y no me decidí a morir ni a rendirme
y gritando les menté a su madre.

Tiempos aquellos: morir, casi una tarea,
por eso acostumbré el paladar al café:
3 ó 300 tazas amargas en La India, en La Prensa
o en cualquier parte, en las vísperas de tu velorio.
A esa hora, la tristeza y la soledad
de quien una vez fue un joven profesor de matemática,

LEONEL RUGAMA
1949-1970

Here I lie, Leonel Rugama Rugama[1],
twice Rugama and hardly of age
(they say twenty is nothing).
I loved the people's circuses
with their tatty mended tents –
sails whipped by the January winds.
Son of a plain schoolteacher
and Pastor Rugama, the carpenter
with his good pot belly, smelling
of cedar sawn in the afternoon.
My soul revisited him as a bullet
grazing one of his legs
in the September insurrection.

I urgently looked for a face,
hers maybe, through all the taxi windows
and speeding urban buses.
But I never saw her
or met her until the end.
When the ammunition ran out
and I pulled the trigger,
face to face there at last she was.
I did not decide to die or surrender,
I shouted at them about their mother.

In those days dying was almost a duty
so I accustomed my palate to coffee
3 or 300 bitter cupfuls in La India,
La Prensa, wherever, keeping vigil for you.
At that hour the lonely gloom
of one who was once a young maths teacher

que anda a salto de mata,
se te suelta en poemas que son puñetazos.
A esa hora uno mismo dicta sus epitafios
y no carga luto –
tu camisola requeneta y tus zapatos tenis.

Clandestino hasta en eso
y clandestino además como seminarista: nunca
vestí la sotana de casimir
con el fajón azul-celeste
ni clericalmente me llevé
las manos al pecho en misa.
No atribuyan más esto a mi humor negro,
pero un buen cristiano calza exacto en un marxista
y ambos, en un 'sandino-comunista'
– como nos motejó *Novedades* al siguiente día
del deslumbre aquel, del enfrentamiento.

El sandinismo es la práctica nicaragüense
del cristianismo.
El Espíritu Santo es el soplo, el aliento,
el ímpetu de la Revolución; es clamor de siglos:
'Envía, Señor, tu Espíritu
y transformarás la faz de la tierra.'
Ustedes, Católicos de pipiripago, Puetillas-managuas,
que no socaron ni creyeron en nada ni en nadie,
sólo Estelí, mi Estelí prenatal
y *post-mortem* supo
que el Hijo del Carpintero llegó hasta ella
y nos recibió y creyó
que sólo después de la Semana Santa de 1979
pudo darse la Revolución, la Resurrección:
jueves 19 de julio
que se adelanta en Domingo de Pascua.

and now plays hide and seek,
breaks out in poems as good as punches.
At that hour you dictate your own epitaphs
and do not wear mourning –
your stocky vest and your tennis shoes.

Clandestine also in this.
I was even a clandestine seminarian:
I never wore the fine wool cassock
with its sky blue sash,
nor did I clerically raise
my hands to my breast at mass.
Don't call it my black humour,
but a good christian fits exactly into a marxist
and both into a 'Sandino-communist'
– as *Novedades* dubbed us
the day after that affray, the confrontation.

Being a Sandinista is the Nicaraguan way
of being a christian.
The Holy Spirit is the wind blowing, breath,
drive of the Revolution, the cry of the ages:
'Lord send forth your Spirit
and transform the face of the earth.'
You pathetic catholics, you Managua poetasters,
who stood for nothing and no one,
only Estelí realised, my pre-birth,
post-mortem Estelí,
that the Carpenter's Son got there
and welcomed us, knowing
that not till after Holy Week 1979
could the Revolution happen, Resurrection:
Thursday the 19th of July
advancing to Easter Day.

OSCAR TURCIOS
1942-1973

Ninguna aristocracia, ninguna
oligarquía, ningún grupo dominante
tuvo jamás un club tan exclusivo
            como él de nosotros.
Para entrar entonces al Frente Sandinista
había que colgar en la percha la vida
            y yo
      allí la vida les dejé.

OSCAR TURCIOS[1]
1942-1973

No aristocracy, no
oligarchy, no ruling class
ever belonged to such an exclusive club
   as we did.
To get into the Sandinista Front then
you had to hang your life up
on the rack and there it was
  that I left mine
    to them for good.

Ricardo Morales, one of the FSLN's leading writers, who fell in combat at Nandaime on 18th September 1973 together with Oscar Turcios.

Arlen Siu

ARLEN SIU

Hija de chinos
comerciantes y restauranteros
en puertos y Jinotepes de Nicaragua,
nací, viví, canté, combatí,
pulsé la guitarra por esta tierra
y como la más nicaragüense
de los nicaragüenses
ningún dolor
me fue ajeno.
Mi sangre arraigó en este suelo
(caí en ese tazón de jade
que es la montaña.
La muerte es una mariposa negra
que te baja los párpados).

Recuérdenme cuando
tras el bambú
de hojas finas como lanzas
se detenga una luna
nítida, lánguida.

ARLEN SIU

Daughter of Chinese[1]
traders and restaurant people
in Nicaragua's ports and Jinotepes,
I was born, lived, sang, fought
and thrummed my guitar for this country
and like the most Nicaraguan
of Nicaraguans
no pain
was alien to me.
My blood watered this soil
(I fell in that jade bowl
which is the mountain.
Death is a black butterfly
lowering your eyelids).

Remember me
when behind the bamboo
with its lance-thin leaves
hangs a languid
brilliant moon.

SATELITE-ASOSOSCA

A Paulino Castellón,
quien me contó este poema.

Remontando la nueva carretera a León,
sobre las luces de la Refinería
y la laguna de Asososca, con Managua
y su lago de fondo, hay un semáforo intermitente
bombeando una luz roja que se refleja
en el asfalto remojado de un domingo ya oscureciendo.

Aquí, donde rebota la luz cayó exactamente;
aquí estuvo o estará destapada para siempre
una de nuestras más hermosas cabezas.
Eduardo Contreras venía para mi casa
y aunque nunca, jamás llegó, nosotros
seguiremos esperándolo, acaso hasta el día
en que cese este sístole y diástole; acaso
hasta el día en que el rojo del semáforo
deje de reavivar y rebotar en luz
la más transparente de las sangres.

THE ASOSOSCA TRAFFIC LIGHT

To Paulino Castellón,
who told me this story

Along the new road to León,
above the bright lit Refinery
and the Asososca lagoon –
background Managua with its Lake –
a traffic light intermittently
changes to red which reflects
on the wet asphalt of a Sunday dusk.

Exactly where its glow falls
there fell forever one of our dearest,
Eduardo Contreras[1] on his way to my house.
Although he never arrived,
we go on expecting him perhaps till the day
when this systole and diastole fails,
till the day maybe
when that red ruby lustre
stops bouncing back at us, revived,
the fresh blood of one of our best.

Managua, 17th November 1980

LA HISTORIA ES COMO
EL CADÁVER DE C.F.

Varias veces han dado por muerto
a Carlos Fonseca:
en El Chaparral, allá por 1959,
un tiro de M-1 en el pulmón;
en Nandaime, allá por septiembre de 73;
en Zinica, allá por noviembre de 1976.
        Pero siempre,
en el preciso momento en que lo van a enterrar
o en el instante en que la GN,
el CONDECA o la zopilotera
se dispone al despojo
de su ropa, de sus botas,
de su mochila
        o de su carabina,
     el cadáver
comienza a dar señales de vida:
aspiración y expiración, vaho, aliento
que se va convirtiendo en neblina,
en esa niebla cerrada que sube
de las montañas de Nicaragua
       cada amanecer.

México, D.F., 7 de octubre de 1977.

HISTORY IS LIKE THE CORPSE
OF CARLOS FONSECA

Several times they announced
the death of Carlos Fonseca:[1]
in El Chaparral back in 1959,
an M-1 bullet in his lung;
in Nandaime in September 73;
November 1976 in Zinica.
                        But always,
just when they are about to bury him
or just when the National Guard,
the CONDECA[2] or the buzzardry
are squabbling over his clothes,
his boots, his kitbag
                or his gun,
                    the corpse
begins to show signs of life:
breathing in and out, breath, vapour
that turns into mist,
the thick fog that lifts
off the mountains of Nicaragua
              every dawn.

Mexico, 7th October 1977

LAPIDA PARA LOS MARTIRES DE SOLENTINAME

HABLA LA GARZA

Soy una Garza de cemento erguida
sobre un túmulo en medio de una placita
que parece agua muerta o tranquila,
frente al Cuartel de San Carlos.
Mientras el Lago golpee tablas
y zancos de las casas de tambo,
y chayules y lanchas invadan todos
los martes al puerto; mientras
la luna florezca como una oropéndola
sobre Solentiname y el Río San Juan
tome impulso en busca del mar,
yo estaré aquí señalando el sitio
donde remansan Donald Guevara,
Felipe Peña y Elvis Chavarría,
muchachos que en la plena madrugada
del 13 de octubre de 1977,
hicieron amanecer más temprano que nunca.

MEMORIAL FOR THE MARTYRS
OF SOLENTINAME

THE HERON SPEAKS

I am a stone heron erected
over a tomb in a square,
which seems a calm backwater
facing the San Carlos Barracks.[1]
While the Lake laps planks
and stilts of the shoreside houses
and mosquitoes and launches
invade the port every Tuesday,
while the moon like a golden oriole
hovers over Solentiname
and the Río San Juan makes for the sea,
I stand here marking the place
where Donald Guevara, Felipe Peña [2]
and Elvis Chavarría now lie still,
lads who in that 1977 dawn
of the Thirteenth of October
made day break earlier than ever.

Felipe Peña

121

CANTAR AL MARGEN DE UNA CAPTURA

Cuando escribo o pronuncio su nombre completo,
un poema o una declaración de amor
se me asoma y esconde, se me escabulle a mí
entre el Doris y el María, entre el Dorismaría.
Pero verla en estas fotos de *La Prensa*, rumbo
al despacho del Juez Unico de Somoto
– remoto y cordillera cómo me viene este pueblo
de Nicaragua – a través de una valla de tenientes
de bigotín y ray-ban,
custodios, jeep, orejas y ojos,
con soltura de himno que despliega su verdad,
con ese rostro suyo en que entrevimos
a la muchacha que amamos. Verla así, digo,
es para desparramar
desde nuestro machismo histórico,
una canción avergonzada.
¡Carajo! cuánta mujer
reincide en una mujer, en una única mujer
que es un coro de mujeres claras en la noche
de abril y su luna, solas con el baqueano
atravesando muertes y madrugadas
hasta ganar la tierra prometida a su rabia.
Motín de mujer. Peso completo de mujer
y unas libras más de la cuenta, ajena
a las dietas del Coca-colonizaje, así de gordita
como podría ser un volcán adolescente. Muchacha
de tamaño nacional que a sí misma se porta
y con ovarios. Por esto las manos del torturador
con ese olor repugnante
de Old Spice en la mañana
la escudriñaron, se los querían arrancar,

SINGING A CAPTURE

When I write or say her full name,
a poem or declaration of love
sneaks out, escapes me
between Doris and Maria, between Dorismaria.[1]
But in those *La Prensa* photos
on her way to the chambers
of the Single Judge of Somoto –
that remote and mountainous
town of Nicaragua – through a hedge
of Ray-Banned,[2] moustached lieutenants,
guards, jeeps, spies and eyes,
we see her confident as a soaring song,
that face of hers giving us a glimpse
of the girl we love. I tell you
seeing her like that shames
our historical machismo
into an outburst of praise.
Wow! what a lot of woman in one,
a single woman who is a bright chorus of women
on a moonlit night in April,
alone with the guide trailing death and dawn
till they reach the land their anger claims.
An insurrection of a woman! A woman full weight
and a few pounds over, alien
to Coca-colonisation diets, plump
as an adolescent volcano. A girl
of national size who takes care of herself,
she's got guts,[3] ovaries. That's why
the torturer's hands with their repugnant
morning smell of Old Spice scrabbled
among them, wanted to tear them out,

enfermizamente la desgarraron. Es cierto,
los cables internacionales lo confirman:
la capturan, mas no le encuentran nada
ni le sacan nada. Cantó y canta, pero es otro
su canto. Nunca será requisada Doris María.
Nunca han visto irreductible su cara.
Arrasada por la libertad y tras la reja, ñata,
la cara. Por fin la GN comete todo un acierto:
métanla en el bunker, métanla en los sótanos,
porque qué dichosamente peligroso es encarcelar
a Doris María Tijerino Haslam, esa
ñata linda que es un racimo de bombas de tiempo.

México, D.F., 23 de abril de 1978

sickeningly ripped her up. It is certain,
international telegrams confirm:
they capture her, but find nothing on her,
get nothing out of her. She sang and sings
but to a different tune.
They will never get Doris Maria;
they never saw her face crumble.
Her snub nose sniffing for freedom
from behind the grating, her face.
In the end the GN[4] get the bright idea
of putting her in the bunker, putting her in cellars,
because fortunately it is dangerous
to imprison Doris Maria Tijerino Haslam,
that lovely snub-nosed woman
who is a cluster of time bombs.

Mexico, 23rd April 1978

ERNESTO CASTILLO SALAVERRY
1957–1978

Jamás me sentí solo
ni en el cuarto de mi casa
donde me acompañaba
tu ausencia como una canción
triste y terca.
Ni en el Instituto Químico de Barcelona
ni en Costa Rica.

Durante el entrenamiento en Cuba
tuve hermanos, compañeros
y cuando salté a las calles
a levantar barricadas
y agitar a León
en la insurección de septiembre,
me rocé, anduve codo a codo con la Muerte.

Hasta mi fosa es una fosa común
cerca del Hospital San Vicente.
Ni en vida ni muerte estuve solo
y menos ya en Revolución,
sólo vos nunca quisiste estar conmigo
ni siquiera dejaste tu nombre
inscrito sobre mi lápida.

ERNESTO CASTILLO SALAVERRY[1]
1957–1978

I never felt alone,
even at home in my room
your absence was with me
like a sad insistent song.
Even in the Barcelona
Chemical Institute,
even in Costa Rica.

During training in Cuba
I had brothers, comrades,
and when I leapt onto the streets
to build barricades and rouse León
in the September insurrection,
I brushed against Death
who walked at my side.

Even my grave is a common one
near the San Vicente Hospital.
I was not alone in life or death,
much less so in Revolution.
Only you never wished to be with me
and did not even leave your name
inscribed on my tomb.

Sandinista combatants in Matagalpa.

And in Estelí.

POR AQUELLAS CALLES DE ESTELI

'Por aquellas calles que yo recorrí para salir, ví más de cien personas muertas a punto de reventar. Entre los muertos se reconocen niños, ancianos, jóvenes y mujeres. El hedor es insoportable; pero se tiene que respirar . . .'.

LA PRENSA, Managua, 21 de noviembre de 1978.

Por aquellas calles de Estelí el tufo es insoportable,
el hedor sube al cielo, y se tiene que respirar
hondo, aspirar, pero expirar, jamás; morirnos, nunca.
Son pilas de cadáveres, más de cien personas:
niños, mujeres enseñando, las pobres, sus piernas,
viejitos, jóvenes bocabajo con los pómulos contra el pavimento
y bocarriba con los brazos desgobernados
y los dientes secos por los labios entreabiertos,
bluyines pesados de sangre y meada póstuma,
zapatos por allá y gafas por aquí, pantorrillas
chamuscadas, cacho-quemado, con el ruedo roto,
pegado, aferrado a la carne roja, casi viva.
Aquello parece más negro, hierve de moscas.
El calor infla las barrigas. Están a punto de reventar
        soplados los muertos,
van a romper las camisas, se les va a brotar la boñiga,
        la chanfaina, la murundanga,
cuando hagan puaff empezará a crecer en sus cuerpos el mundo.

THROUGH THOSE ESTELI STREETS[1]

'In those Estelí streets I walked through to get out I saw more than a hundred dead persons, corpses on the point of exploding. Among the dead there were children, old people, young people and women. The stench is unbearable but one has got to breathe.'

LA PRENSA, Managua, 21 November 1978

In those Estelí streets the stench is unbearable,
the smell rises to heaven, and you've got to breathe
deeply, respire, but never expire; never say die.
There are piles of corpses, more than a hundred people,
children, poor women showing their legs,
old and young face down with cheeks to the pavement,
face up with their arms splayed,
teeth dry in their gaping mouths,
jeans sodden with blood and posthumous piss,
shoes here, glasses over there, charred
calves, burnt bone, ripped skirts
stick, cling to almost alive raw skin.
That one looks blacker, teems with flies.
Heat swells stomachs. They are about to explode,
      the dead will blow
up, burst through shirts, spurt dung, guts, offal.
When they go off, in their bodies the world
      will start to grow.

ALEJANDRO DAVILA BOLAÑOS
1922-1979

Fui uno de los primeros bolcheviques de Masaya,
pero pasé mi vida entre Estelí
y las cárceles somocistas
donde crecieron mi barba negra, mi barba gris
y mi frondosa barba cana,
la misma que me agarraron los guardias
enloquecidos con Imipramina y marihuana
para arrancarme del quirófano.

Médicos y enfermeras fuimos pasto
en la Operación Limpieza.
Estelí aún ardía por el bombardeo
y nosotros empezamos a arder en gasolina.
Apenas se oían uno que otro tiro,
una ráfaga postrera, una consigna lejana.
El viento de la tarde dispersó las cenizas
quedando sólo mis anteojos
y otros cuerpos reducidos, achicharrados.

Pero los muchachos y los guerrilleros
que suturamos lograron romper el cerco.
Lo único que lamento
es que no me sepultaron
en una olla cineraria con los granos de maiz tostado.
Lástima, sin mi pozol
sin mi huacal de chicha fresca
para brindar con todos y por todos los dioses
del cielo nahuatl que yo inventé para mí.

ALEJANDRO DAVILA BOLAÑOS
1922-1979

I was one of the first bolsheviks in Masaya
but I spent my life between Estelí[1]
and Somoza's prisons,
where my black beard grew, my white beard grew
and my bushy old man's beard,
which the guards grabbed – crazed
on Imipramine and marihuana –
to drag me out of the operating theatre.

We doctors and nurses were fodder
in the Clean-up Operation.
With Estelí bombed and burning
we were set alight with petrol.
One shot followed another,
a final burst, a far off shout.
The ashes blew on the afternoon wind,
leaving only my glasses
and other charred corpses.

But the lads and guerrillas we sutured
managed to break the siege.
The only thing I lament
is that they did not bury me
in a funeral pot with roasted maize.
What a pity to be without my *pozol*[2]
without my *huacal* of cold *chicha*
to toast them, with and by
all the gods of my Nahuatl sky.

GERMAN POMARES

Me madrugaron.
Caer y a las puertas de la Ciudad
(ya se divisaban los techos y las luces de Jinotega).
¡Puta! En la boca del horno quemárseme el pan.
Morir es desertar de la columna
y yo no me voy,
aquí me muero
y vuelvo muy al alba a la tierra;
me hago polvo, hectárea,
lodazal, parcela, potrero.

Que el INRA, Compañeros,
reparta y comparta,
siembre y germine este cuerpo mío
hecho ya tierra de mi tierra.

GERMAN POMARES[1]

They cheated me .
To fall at the city gates
(in sight of Jinotega's roofs and lights)
burning my bread at the oven door!
Dying is deserting the column
and I am not going,
I die here but I'll be back
to earth before daybreak.
I will be soil, acre,
bog, field, pasture.

Comrades let INRA[2]
distribute and share me,
land in my land now let my body
be sown and germinate.

RAFAELA PADILLA

Yo iba al hospital clandestino
allá por el viejo Cine Fénix de Masaya,
a ponerle suero a un combatiente
herido en el Repliegue.
Y allí los guardias
me quebraron como se desguapa una tinaja
a culata y patadas.
Por las gradas del colegio
aquella tarde se derramó
mi pelo liso negro y mi sangre.

Aún me resisto a los golpes, a la muerte,
a no atender al enfermo, a dejar
a mis muchachitos sin madre.
Médicos, Enfermeras, Personal Hospitalario,
Compañeros: el antiguo dolor humano
es nuevo, distinto,
intransferible en cada paciente.
Recuerden ésto. Ténganlo presente siempre.

RAFAELA PADILLA

I was going to the clandestine hospital
by the old Phoenix Cinema in Masaya
to give serum to a combatant
wounded in the Retreat.[1]
There the guards
smashed me like a clay pot
with kicks and blows from their rifle butts.
Over the college steps that afternoon
spread a pool of my blood
and my sleek black hair.

I still resist blows, death,
I mind not minding the sick,
leaving my children motherless.
Hospital workers, Doctors, Nurses,
Comrades: our ancient human pain
is new, different and untransferable
in every patient. Remember that.
Don't ever forget.

EPISTOLA AL CAPITAN LAUREANO MAIRENA, JEFE DE GUARDAFRONTERAS EN EL NORTE

Que alegre, Laureano habernos hallado
anoche en la Casa del Padre: 10 años de no vernos,
desde aquel diciembre de 1970
hasta este mayo de 1981.
10 años son una vida muchas vidas y muertes,
la tuya, la mía y todas revueltas, encontradas
en una sola corriente.

Es tanto tiempo como el que media
entre nuestras barbas y bigotes actuales
y los rostros ya perdidos de la adolescencia,
como la distancia que hay del archipiélago
al puertecito de San Carlos
(Trecho que vos cruzabas en la SAN JUAN DE LA CRUZ
erguido en la proa, botas de hule y cotona blanca,
con tus crenchas rubias al aire, riéndote,
rompiendo y retando la recia tumbazón,
en feliz y temerario gobierno de la barca).

Turbio y claro veo el paisaje, esa época, distante
y cercano como tu brazo alargándome
desde el muelle de tablas
hasta la SANTA ANA – la lancha –
media botella de ron
                    para la larga travesía larga.
Vos nos viniste a dejar ese viernes.
Yo había llegado con dos señores salesianos
en proyecto de regeneración a Solentiname
(y te advierto que los dos están con la Revolución.
                    Se salvaron).

LETTER TO CAPTAIN LAUREANO MAIRENA, CHIEF OF THE BORDER GUARD IN THE NORTH

How lovely, Laureano[1],
to have met last night in the Father's[2] house:
after ten years, from that December
in 1970 till this May 1981.
Ten years are a lifetime, so many lives and deaths,
yours, mine and all tumbled together
in a single stream.

Such a long time measured
by our present moustaches, beards
and our lost adolescent faces.
Like the distance between the archipelago
and the little port of San Carlos
(a stretch you crossed in the SAN JUAN DE LA CRUZ
standing at the prow in your white shirt and gumboots,
your fair curls in the wind, laughing
as you faced and fought the swell,
daring the boat, enjoying your mastery).

I see the country cloudy and clear,
that time far off and near
like your arm stretched out to help me
from the plank jetty onto the SANTA ANA –
the launch – with half a bottle of rum
for the lengthy crossing.
You came to see us off that Friday.
I had arrived with two Salesian gentlemen
seeking regeneration at Solentiname
(and I can tell you that both are with the Revolution.
They were saved).

Esa mañana, cuando dejé la Comunidad
supe llorar y no dejarme ver;
supe que William y vos,
la Teresita y su Juan tierno, tuntuneco,
Alejandro y el Poeta estaban en lo cierto en aquella
noche oscura del alma y del cuerpo de Nicaragua.

Ninguna abadía del mundo, ni la de Notre Dame en Grace,
ni la antigua cartuja
de *Le Reposoir, Haute-Savoie*
podía como Nuestra Señora de Solentiname
hacerse a la contemplación
lo mismo que península mar adentro, con palmas
y garzas, azules del aire y del agua,
cocos y racimos de mangos,
zanates y guapotes
cuya sola existencia es un canto.

El Poeta había tenido su nuevo Pentecostés en Cuba
y andaba la lengua más suelta que de costumbre
y si yo me hubiera quedado con Ustedes,
hoy no sería este miope aprendiz de filología,
y tal vez tendría la palma de los mártires
(tengo con Ustedes, pues, esta deuda).

Todos Ustedes eran hombres de Dios, empeñados en su pesca.
      Puritas Cordis era la regla.
Las órdenes mayores y menores
nunca alcanzaron tal contemplación.
Me dice el Poeta que estás en el Norte.
Sos Jefe de los Guardafronteras, guardás
el límite entre Nicaragua y los ex GN,
allá donde limita el cielo de esta tierra con el infierno.

That morning, when I left the Community
I cried and let no one see;
I knew that William and you,
Teresita and her tender, tottery Juan,
Alejandro and the Poet were certainly in that
dark night of Nicaragua's soul and body.

No abbey in the world, not Our Lady in Grace,
not the ancient charterhouse
of *Le Reposoir, Haute Savoie,*
lent itself to contemplation
as did Our Lady of Solentiname,
like a peninsula out to sea with palm trees
and herons, air and water blues,
coconuts, mangoes,
grackles and cichlid fish
whose very existence is a song.

The Poet had had his new Pentecost in Cuba
and his tongue was looser than usual
and if I'd stayed with you, today I wouldn't be
this short-sighted philology student,
and perhaps I'd bear the martyrs' palm
(so with you I have this debt).

You were all God's folk, engaged in his fishing.
    Puritas Cordis was the rule.
Such contemplation was never attained.
by the major and minor orders.
The Poet tells me you are in the North.
You are the Chief Border Guard, guarding
the frontier between Nicaragua and the ex-GN,[3]
where this earth's heaven meets hell.

Dice que a cada ratito te metés hasta la línea de fuego,
o sea, seguís atravesando el lago
bajo nubarrones y sobre chubascos, de pie siempre
sobre la proa enrumbado
hacia las más alta contemplación,
        hasta la más alta.

Managua, mayo de 1981

He says that you constantly get in the line of fire,
or rather you go on crossing the lake,
beneath storm cloud and squall
you stand at the prow and steer
course for the highest contemplation,
    the highest of all.

Managua, May 1981

YO TENIA UN SOBRINO

Yo tenía un sobrino un poquito mayor en edad
que el triúnfo de la Revolución.
La insurgencia de septiembre la pasó en buen refugio;
pero después, era de verlo, no había acabado de nacer
cuando empezó a pegar cuatro gritos por el mundo,
con los puños cerrados como bombitas de contacto.

Para la Ofensiva Final ya era un experto
en tirarse con su madre debajo de las camas,
en replegarse al pecho de Doña Ermida, al fin abuela,
o en cruzar noches cerradas
de rockets y morteros.
Gordo, feo el chamaco jodido,
lindo como una tanqueta Sherman recién recuperada
            a la Guardia,
avanzaba arrebatando días solares a la muerte.

La Revolución y él se iban poniendo hermosos,
            pijuda la pareja,
pero al sobrino me le dio un sarampión marca infierno.
Ojalá que a la Revolución no me le pase nada,
no me le va a suceder nada, aunque vengan epidemias,
aunque el vecindario esté infecto, se le está cuidando,
            poniéndole las vacunas.
Estamos locos con Ella
dándole las medicinas a su tiempo.

I HAD A NEPHEW

I had a nephew a bit older
than the triumph of the Revolution.
He spent the September insurrection snug
but after that, he was something else!
No sooner born than he shouts and screams
clenching his fists like little contact bombs.

For the Final Offensive he became expert
at shooting under beds with his mother,
retreating to Doña Ermida's breast –
a granny at last – or nights beneath
rockets and mortar shells.
Fat and ugly, the awful child,
pretty as a Sherman tank
just captured from the Guard,
advanced snatching sunlit days from death.

The Revolution and he began to look better,
handsome the pair of them,
but my nephew got a nasty bout of measles.
Let's hope the Revolution won't catch anything,
that nothing goes wrong. Even if epidemics come
and the neighbourhood gets infected,
we are taking care to vaccinate.
We are besotted with her,
giving her all her medicines at the right time.

ASI ES LA COSA

'Los hombres ya reclaman, como derecho inalienable, establecer aqui
en la tierra, su reino celeste.'

ENRIQUE HEINE

No jodan, si aquí en Nicaragua las estrellas
están al alcance de las manos.
Las Siete Cabritas que suben y bajan
y brillan y brincan
sobre el Cerro de Catarina,
las Pupilas de Santa Lucía,
los Vértices del Arado
te las puedes meter en la bolsa de reloj
o de la camisa.

Claro está que costó y cuestan
un ojo de la cara,
un güevo y la mitad del otro,
medio Masaya, León y medio,
Estelí entera,
pero logramos bajar el cielo
a la tierra.

Managua-Masaya, noviembre de 1979

THAT'S THE WAY IT IS

'Human beings claim the inalienable right to establish their kingdom of heaven here on earth.'

H. HEINE

Fuck it, it's true, here in Nicaragua
the stars are within handreach,
the Seven Sisters rising and setting,
winking and twinkling
over the Catarina Hills,
St Lucy's Pupils
and the points of the Plough,
tuck them in your watch pocket
or your shirt.

Naturally it cost.
They cost an eye from the face,
one ball and half the other,
half Masaya, León and a half,
the whole of Estelí,
but we managed to fetch heaven
down to earth.

Managua-Masaya, November 1979

TOQUE

Las campanas de la Parroquia
de Nuestra Señora de la Asunción de Masaya,
sólo serían campanas y nada más
que campanas si permanecieran calladas.
Todo es que empiecen a repicar
para que se conviertan en ángeles
y querubines gordos muy niños,
meciéndose peligrosamente en la torre,
enseñando sus piernas y nalgotas
mientras dan vuelo a su cotón metálico
sobre las antiguas tejas de barro.

Como multiplican estas campanas la claridad
de estos primeros domingos del verano.
        Ya es noviembre
y los árboles de mango y guayaba están cargados
de una luz que es más,
mucho más que hojas y agua.
Aquí y ahora. A estas alturas,
a las nueve y cuarto de la mañana
            no es posible la muerte.

La vida es más rotunda que nunca,
apenas el grito lejano del vende periódico
confirma que no hay contrarrevolución que valga.
En los camiones IFA el mundo se levanta y anda
coreando consignas. Son los milicianos
que vienen del lado del panteón; oigan
sus voces entre el día y las campanas,
salgamos a la puerta, a la calle
todos los caídos retornan, han resucitado.

PEALING BELLS

The parish bells
of Our Lady of the Assumption in Masaya[1]
would be just bells and nothing more
if they stayed dumb.
But when they start pealing
they become angels,
fat cherub children
rocking dangerously in the tower
showing their legs and bums
and fluttering their metallic shirts
over the ancient roof tiles.

How these bells sharpen the clarity
of those first summer Sundays.
                Now it is November
and the mango and guava trees laden
with a light that is more,
much more than leaves and water.
Here and now. At this height
at a quarter past nine in the morning
        death is not possible.

Life is rounder than ever.
Faintly the far off cry of the paper seller
confirms that there is no real counter-revolution.
In the IFA[2] lorries the world gets up and goes
carrying orders. The militiamen come
from the pantheon side; listen
to their voices mingling with bells and daylight.
Go to the door, outside in the street
all the fallen return, have risen again.

149

NOTES

These notes providing some background details to the songs and poems are necessarily sketchy. Much of the information has been gathered orally – appropriate to the epic genre but the translator apologises if mistakes have crept in. The most readily available popular history of the Nicaraguan Revolution is George Black's *Triumph of the People. The Sandinista Revolution in Nicaragua* (Zed Press, London 1981).

CANTO EPICO TO THE FSLN

Nicaragua Nicaragüita

1. 'Nicaragüita' is also the name of the national flower, frangipani (*plumeria*).
2. Diriangén was an Indian chief who resisted the Spanish conquistadors in the sixteenth century.

Sandino

1. 'Jiñocuago' (*bursera simarouba*): the 'gumbo limbo' is a tree with soft bark which the Indians wrote their stories on.
2. 'Malinche' (*poinciana regia*, called 'flamboyant' or 'flame tree' in the Caribbean) has bright red flowers and rattling pods, used as musical instruments, which are shaped like machetes.
3. Sandino is usually called 'Augusto César Sandino'. He is called Calderón here because that was his mother's surname.
4. 'Sacuanjoche' from the Aztec *zacuani xochitl* = 'yellow flower' (*plumeria*): frangipani is Nicaragua's national flower, also called 'nicaragüita'.

The Abduction

1. 'Gongolona' is also the name of a bird.
2. 'Mozote' (*cenchrus echinatus*): a sandbur. From the Aztec *motzoloa*: 'to stick fast'.

The Birth

1. The orginal Mayan inhabitants of Nicaragua were 'people made of maize'. Maize is still very important as a staple Nicaraguan crop and food (in 'tortillas' : maize pancakes).

The Trees

1. Not all the blessings given by the trees are sung on the cassette. However perhaps we should assume that they are speaking in tree language. For example rosewood is used to make the marimba and at the point in the

song where it is said to give its blessing ('your laugh will ring sweet as marimba...'), we hear not words but – the marimba!

2. Ceiba (*ceiba pentandra*): the ceiba or silk cotton tree, which produces kapok.

3. 'Malinche' (*poinciana regia*, called 'flamboyant' or 'flame tree' in the Caribbean). Its blessing 'your flower will flame for the humble, the mighty you'll mortally wound' accords with its bright red flowers followed by large pods shaped like machetes.

4. 'Chilamate' (*ficus laurifolia* literally 'laurel-leafed fig' but it does not produce figs): common Nicaraguan tree with twisty trunk.

5. *Tayacán* is an Indian word for a chief or leader.

6. 'Jocote' (*spondias*): the hog plum. The type known as 'tronador' ('thunderer') crackles loudly when it is bitten.

7. 'Espabel' (*anarcardium excelsum*): the wild cashew.

8. Granadillo, also called rosewood, is the wood used to make the marimba, an instrument like a giant wooden xylophone with hanging resonance pipes.

9. 'Jenizaro' (*pithecolobium saman*): a large spreading tree, the 'raintree'.

10. 'Jicaro' (*crescencia cujete*): the calabash tree. Calabashes grow on it and their seeds are used to make a cold drink.

11. The 'ten' are the ten founders of the FSLN who were: Carlos Fonseca, Tomás Borge, Silvio Mayorga, Santos López, Jorge Navarro, Francisco Buitrago, Rigoberto Cruz (Pablo Ubeda), José Benito Escobar, Faustino Ruiz, and Germán Pomares ('The Tapir'). Only Tomás Borge is still alive and is now Nicaraguan Minister of the Interior.

Raití-Bocay

1. Three of the FSLN's founders died in these actions:

Jorge Navarro who had conducted the *Frente*'s first bank raid, obtaining 35,000 cordobas ($5000).

Faustino Ruiz ('El Cuje': 'The Sparrowhawk') who 'never held out his hand except to give something, kind and sweet as the cashew nut, which always keeps its heart on the outside.'

Francisco Buitrago, who had worked with Carlos Fonseca in the student movement since the fifties.

Others who died at Raití-Bocay were: Iván Sanchez, Boanerges Santamaria, Modesto Duarte.

2. Tuneros: Workers with 'tuna', the prickly pear (*opuntia*). Also used, as here, for 'hulero': 'rubber tapper'.

3. Wankí: Miskito name for the Rio Coco.

Pablo Ubeda

1. 'Mozote' (*cenchrus echinutus*): a sandbur.

2. A *mesta* judge was a local National Guard official.
3. The *cadejo* is a strange mythical animal who appears suddenly and alarmingly, especially at night, and then disappears - a figure of mystery and terror to the superstitious country sergeant. To be like the *cadejo* means to be someone everybody talks about but no one has seen.

Pancasán

1. Losses were heavy at Pancasán. Those who died included Silvio Mayorga, Rigoberto Cruz (Pablo Ubeda) and Carlos Reyna (see previous song), Oscar Danilo Rosales, Nicholas Sánchez, Francisco Moreno, Otto Casco, Fausto García, Felipe Gaitán, Fermin Díaz, Carlos Tinoco, Ernesto Fernández and Oscar Armando Florez.
2. Silvio Mayorga had been with Carlos Fonseca since their student days in León and was at the 1961 Tegucigalpa meeting with him and Tomás Borge to set up what became the FSLN. He fought at Patuca in 1961 and was one of the leaders of the Raití-Bocay actions in 1963.

Julio Buitrago

1. As well as the five killed, two militants were captured and tortured, one being Doris Tijerino, now head of the police.
2. The words 'The heroes did not say that they were dying . . . ' are from a poem by Leonel Rugama, 'The Houses were filled with Smoke.'

Leonel Rugama

1. When the Guard called upon him to surrender Leonel replied with the (very Latin) super-insult expressing total defiance: 'Let your mother surrender!' Leonel's mother and aunt now keep a bookshop in Estelí and told the translator he did what he did 'because he had such a good education'.
   Leonel Rugama's poems are available in *La Tierra es un Satélite de la Luna* (4th ed. Managua 1985).

Carlos Fonseca

1. In 1956 Carlos had formed a marxist group of university students in León with Silvio Mayorga and Tomás Borge. He was imprisoned in September 1956 after Rigoberto Lopez Perez had assassinated the first Somoza. In 1957 he visited Moscow and wrote 'A Nicaraguan in Moscow'. On June 24th 1959 he was seriously wounded in his right lung during a guerrilla action at El Chaparral. Later that year, as a member of the JRN (Nicaraguan Revolutionary Youth), he worked with Nicaraguans employed on the US-owned banana plantations in Costa Rica. In July 1961 together with Silvio Mayorga and Tomás Borge, he set up the organisation which later came to be called the FSLN. In 1962 he did reconnaissance work in the region where the Raití-Bocay guerrilla actions would take place the following year. In 1963 he also worked to gain support for the FSLN inside

Nicaragua. On June 29th 1964 he was captured again and wrote 'From Prison I accuse the Dictatorship'. In 1965 he was exiled for the third time. In 1966 he re-entered Nicaragua clandestinely and started preparing for a guerrilla base in the centre of the country, around Pancasán, where the battle took place the following year. In 1969, the year he was named Secretary General of the FSLN, he was captured in a safe house in Costa Rica in August. On December 23rd a group led by Humberto Ortega attempted to spring him from prison (Ortega was seriously wounded) and on October 21st 1970 a second spectacular attempt, involving a kidnapped Costa Rican plane and led by Carlos Agüero, successfully freed Fonseca, Ortega and others, who flew to Mexico, then Cuba. In prison Fonseca had written 'Zero Hour' (translated in *Sandinistas Speak* (ed. Bruce Marcus, Pathfinder, New York/London 1982). He continued in exile as the FSLN's Secretary General, writing, agitating and also visited Korea and China.

In November 1975 he returned clandestinely to Nicaragua, gave a course to militants in Managua and moved about the country from camp to camp, accompanied by Carlos Agüero, Claudia Chamorro, Francisco Rivera and others, until his death in action in Boca de Piedra, Zinica on November 8th 1976. (From *Carlos: El Eslabon Vital: Cronología Basica de Carlos Fonseca, Jefe de la Revolución* (Institute of Sandinista Studies, Managua 1985).

2. El Danto 'The Tapir': Germán Pomares, see his song below, p. 75.
3. Pedrón: Pedro Altamirano, one of Sandino's generals.
4. Benjamin Zeledón led an early popular resistance movement against the US-controlled government of the conservative Adolfo Díaz in 1912.
5. General Ramón Raudales, a veteran of Sandino's army. Died 1958 in a guerrilla attack on the National Guard, which he had led from the town of Danli across the Honduran border. Most of his troops were young students.
6. Claudia: Claudia Chamorro, an FSLN militant who, with others, accompanied Carlos Fonseca as he moved about the country from March 1976 onwards, until his death on November 8th 1976. Claudia fell in combat at Las Bayas, Jinotega on 9th January 1977.

October

1. Donald Guevara and Elvis Chavarría were members of Ernesto Cardenal's community in Solentiname, an archipelago on Lake Nicaragua. They were both captured after the assault and killed. Chato Medrano (not a member of the Solentiname community) also took part in the assault and was killed. See *El Asalto a San Carlos. Testimonios de Solentiname* (Managua 1986).
2. La Foquita ('Little Seal') was a boy militant and Israel Lewites a Nicaraguan Jewish FSLN militant, whose brother became a Minister in the Sandinista Government.

Comandante Federico

1. With Henry Ruiz ('Modesto'), now Minister of Planning, and Tomás Borge, now Minister of the Interior, Pedro Arauz was one of the leaders of the 'Prolonged Popular War' (GPP) tendency of the FSLN.

Camilo Ortega

1. 'Pitahaya' is a liana with brilliant red flowers.

The Assault on the Palace

1. In this operation Eden Pastora was 'Comandante 0', Hugo Torres 'Comandante 1' and Dora Maria Tellez 'Comandante 2'.
2. This song was written for the Mexican singer Amparo Ochoa and and the story is told as if heard in Mexico. (Recently it has usually been sung by Enrique Duarte, one of Los de Palacaguina.)
3. Tacho the Kid (El Chigüin): Anastasio (Tacho) Somoza Portocarrero, the last dictator's son and head of the feared and hated EEBI (Basic Infantry Training School), crack National Guard troops.
4. Luis Pallais Debayle was Somoza's cousin, Vice President of the House of Deputies and director of *Novedades* the government newspaper. Panchito Argeñal Papi was a large landowner from León and ardent supporter of Somoza.
5. Tomás: Tomás Borge, one of the founders of the FSLN, now Minister of the Interior. The FSLN had demanded the release of 85 militants (27 never appeared because they had been murdered in prison). As well as Tomás, those released included Charlotte Baltodano, Edgard Lang, Martha Cranshaw, Doris Tijerino and Felipe Peña.
6. A grackle (*quiscalus*) is a common Nicaraguan bird. It is also called 'clarinero' ('bugler') because the song of the male bird sounds like a bugle call.

Matagalpa

1. The Guanuca is a local river.
2. El Tule is a district of Matagalpa
3. *Nixtayol* is maize dough used to make *tortillas*, which is prepared in the small hours at about the time when this star comes out.

Estelí

1. Davila Bolaños was a local doctor killed in Esteli's April 1979 insurrection. See his poem 'Alejandro Davila Bolaños', p. 133.
2. In Estelí's April 1979 insurrection the population turned out to support FSLN *comandante* Francisco Rivera, who led a 200-strong column to occupy the town.

La Concepción Castle

1. Rafaela Herrera was the daughter of the castle guardian during the time of

the war with the 'filibuster' Walker (1955-7) who, with US-support, attempted to take possession of Nicaragua for himself. Rafaela repelled the invading North American ships by placing burning timbers across the Rio San Juan. 'Enlightened' ('iluminada') is therefore a pun.

2. Ivan Montenegro, one of the senior leaders of the the Southern Front, led the Jacinto Hernández Column and was killed in the action on May 17th 1979.

3. This verse is not on the cassette. It is printed in italics as it goes together with the next verse which is spoken and therefore also in italics.

4. Mancarrón and La Cigueña: islands on Lake Nicaragua in the Solentiname archipelago where Ernesto Cardenal had his christian community.

5. Felipe Peña was a member of the Solentiname community who took part in the assault on San Carlos Barracks on 13th October 1977. (See 'October'). He was captured, released with other prisoners after the Assault on the National Palace, then joined the Nueva Guinea Front and was killed shortly before the Triumph on July 19th 1979.

6. Adolfo García Barbarena, killed in the action on May 17th 1979. Nicaraguans like to eat mangoes in hard slices seasoned with salt.

El Danto: The Tapir

1. The eighty who attacked El Jicaro comprised members of all three FSLN 'tendencies', which had now united in a strategy for victory. The tendencies were the 'Prolonged Popular War', the 'Proletarian' and the 'Insurrectional' or Tercerista (Third), whose policy prevailed.

2. The common English name for the 'lion bird' is 'squirrel cuckoo'. 'Lion bird' is the literal translation of 'pajaro león', given this name because it 'roars'. It also occurs in the song 'Carlos Fonseca'.

León Cathedral

1. The famous Nicaraguan poet Rubén Darío is buried here.

2. On 23rd July 1959 the National Guard massacred students on a demonstration in León. (Sergio Ramirez, the present vice-president, was one of the students on this demonstration.)

3. On 26th September 1956 the poet Rigoberto Lopez Perez assassinated the first Somoza in León .

4. The 21 is a prison.

5. The Acosasco is a fort a short distance from the city.

6. Lupe Moreno and Araceli Perez Darias were FSLN militants killed in León. San Felipe is a district of León.

The Retreat

1. Nindirí is a village near Masaya.

2. Santiago is a volcano on the way to Masaya. Somoza used to throw victims into it. In this song the volcano, like all the rest of nature, is supporting the forces of liberation.

The Triumph

1. On 23rd July 1959, exactly twenty years earlier, the National Guard had massacred students on a demonstration in León. July 23rd 1961, when Carlos Fonseca, Tomás Borge and Silvio Mayorga held their meeting in Tegucigalpa, Honduras, is the official birthday of the FSLN.

NICARAGUAN VISION AND OTHER POEMS

Nicaraguan Vision

1. Carlos's full name was Carlos Fonseca Amador so the word 'lover ' here is a play on his last name.

Epitaph for the Fifty Thousand

1. 50,000 Nicaraguans died in the Revolution out of a total population of about 3 million.

Jorge Navarro

1. See 'Raití-Bocay', song p. 19 and note p. 151.

Silvio Mayorga

1. See 'Pancasán', song p. 27 and note p. 152.

Monument for Julio Buitrago

1. See his song p. 35 and note p. 152.
2. OSN: Oficina de Seguridad Nacional: Somoza's Security forces.
3. Garand and Browning are types of gun. A Sherman tank was used in the siege of Julio's safe house in Managua.

Leonel Rugama

1. See his song p. 37 and note p. 152.

Oscar Turcios

1. Oscar Turcios was a member of the FSLN leadership killed together with Ricardo Morales on 18th September 1973, when the National Guard surprised their safe house 'La Ermita' at Nandaime – a village which stands at the intersection of the Panamerican Highway and the main road to Granada.

Arlen Siu

1. Arlen Siu was an FSLN militant of Chinese descent. She was killed in action at El Sauce in 1975, covering her comrades' retreat. She was a poet and singer – her most famous song was 'Maria Rural' about the hardship suffered by Nicaragua's peasant women.

The Asososca Traffic Light

1. See '*Comandante* Marcos', song p. 43.

History is like the Corpse of Carlos Fonseca

1. See 'Carlos Fonseca', song (which drew inspiration from this poem) p. 49 and note p 152.
2. CONDECA, Consejo de Defensa Centroamericana: Central American Defence Council: US-controlled 'counter-insurgency' organisation set up in 1964, which gave strong support to the dictatorship.

Memorial for the Martyrs of Solentiname

1. See 'October', song p. 53 and note p. 153.
2. See note 5 to 'La Concepción Castle', p. 155.

Singing a Capture

1. *Comandante* Doris Maria Tijerino, a veteran FSLN militant, worked with Carlos Fonseca before Pancasán and co-signed with him the FSLN communique 'Sandino Yes, Somoza no, Revolution yes, Electoral farce no' under the pseudonym Conchita Alday. On 15th July 1969 she was captured and tortured by the Guard in the Delicias del Volga attack, in which Julio Buitrago was killed. She was captured in Somoto in the same month as this poem was written, April 1978. She was one of the prisoners released through the Assault on the National Palace on 22nd August 1978. At present she is Nicaragua's Chief of Police. (See also Margaret Randall, *Inside the Nicaraguan Revolution: The Story of Doris Tijerino* (Vancouver 1978).
2. Ray-Banned: Ray-Ban dark glasses were regarded as very posh and much favoured by Somoza's officers.
3. Spanish text only has 'ovaries'. The poet explained that as well as the literal meaning, this was part of 'historical machismo's' confession and he intended 'she's got ovaries' to parallel 'he's got balls (güevos)', a common Nicaraguan expression meaning someone is very brave. 'Guts' seemed about the best English equivalent.
4. GN: National Guard

Ernesto Castillo Salaverry

1. FSLN militant killed in the September insurrection in León. Nephew of Ernesto Cardenal, who wrote a poem for him: 'Poet killed at twenty / I am thinking about what you said Ernesto / now that soldiers are kissing children / and there is a poetry workshop in the Police Station.'

Through those Estelí Streets

1. See 'Estelí', song p. 69 and note p. 154.

Alejandro Davila Bolaños

1. See 'Estelí', song p. 69 and note p. 154. The Estelí hospital is called after Davila Bolaños now. The Scottish midwife Sue Murray and Chilean film maker Hector Fuentes, resident in Estelí, have made a film about life in this hospital, which is available in England from Banana Tapes, Sheffield (Tel. 0742 452968.)
2. *Pozol*: National drink made of maize and sugar.
   Huacal: Goblet made from half a calabash gourd, often finely carved.
   Chicha: Traditional American Indian drink, which may or may not be fermented, usually made of maize, cane juice or palm juice.
   Nahuatl: American Indian language.

Germán Pomares

1. See El Danto, song p. 75.
2. INRA: Nicaraguan Agrarian Reform Institute.

Rafaela Padilla

1. Rafaela Padilla was an FSLN nurse. See also 'The Retreat', song p. 85.

Letter to Captain Laureano Mairena

1. Laureano Mairena was a member of Ernesto Cardenal's Solentiname community, who took part in the assault on San Carlos Barracks on 13th October 1977. (See also 'October' song p. 53 and note p. 153.) As Chief of the Border Guard after the Revolution Laureano was killed in action in 1982.
2. The Father and the Poet are both Ernesto Cardenal, now Minister of Culture. In 1970 he visited Cuba and was so impressed that he referred to it as his 'second conversion'.
3. GN: National Guard.

Pealing Bells

1. The poet Julio Valle-Castillo comes from Masaya. There is an interview with him in Margaret Randall *Risking a Somersault in the Air. Conversations with Nicaraguan Writers* (San Francisco 1984).
2. IFA lorries: lorries imported from the USSR.